This Book Is a Com... Study Guide to the Online Course:

The course is free to all InterNACHI members.

Upon successfully completing the online course and passing the final exam, you will receive a Certificate of Completion and be able to:

- identify and describe specific details of buildings that may cause moisture-related problems;
- describe the design, construction and maintenance of houses and buildings that manage moisture effectively;
- inspect for indications of moisture intrusion;
- communicate how to prevent moisture intrusion by proper installation of systems and components;
- understand how energy, moisture, water and vapor move through a building;
- recognize evidence of structural damage and previous repair; and
- communicate to clients about indications of moisture intrusion.

Take the online course at **www.nachi.org/moisturecourse**

How to Inspect for Moisture Intrusion

This publication is designed primarily for residential and commercial property inspectors who will learn how to inspect for moisture intrusion in buildings and homes. This guide discusses the design, construction, maintenance and other details of homes and buildings in order to assist inspectors in looking for and identifying defects that may cause moisture-related problems, and to help property owners manage moisture effectively. This guide is also a useful reference tool for inspectors on the job, as well as a handy study aid for InterNACHI's *How to Inspect for Moisture Intrusion* online course and exam.

To order additional training books, visit www.InspectorOutlet.com

Authors:

Ben Gromicko, Director of Education, International Association of Certified Home Inspectors
Nick Gromicko, Founder, International Association of Certified Home Inspectors

Graphics:

Lisaira Vega, Levi Nelson, Erica Saurey & Chris Krowiak

Editor:

Kate Tarasenko / Crimea River, LLC

Layout & Design:

Jessica Langer

www.NACHI.org

Table of Contents

Acknowledgements and Foreword

Acknowledgements

This guide draws upon many resources from the building and inspection industries to combine the subjects of moisture intrusion and building practices and standards that make a home moisture-resistant, as well as the methods of inspecting for moisture-related problems, which include judgment, experience and common sense.

Several groups, such as the International Association of Certified Home Inspectors (InterNACHI), the U.S. Department of Housing and Urban Development (HUD) and its Partnership for Advancing Technology in Housing (PATH) Program, the U.S. Department of Energy (DOE), the Canadian Mortgage and Housing Corporation (CHMC), the Engineered Wood Association (APA), and many others listed throughout this publication have all produced useful guidelines and standards for building construction and inspection methods. Some of the content and illustrations in this book can be found in "Moisture-Resistant Homes," a document by the U.S. Department of Housing and Urban Development, and was rewritten and adapted for commercial and home inspectors. Many illustrations come from the "Builder's Foundation Handbook," a document by the U.S. Department of Energy.

Foreword

The proper design and construction of homes and other buildings have always involved attention to moisture control for the straightforward need to keep moisture out and protect the structure from deterioration. In recent years, however, this issue has become much more complex, and property owners' and occupants' expectations have risen. Moisture control now includes the challenge of managing interior moisture, including water vapor, in order to promote the occupants' comfort, protect indoor air quality, and prevent the development of mold.

More than ever before, consumers are demanding better performance from their homes. Total moisture protection for houses is a daunting goal. At the same time, our understanding of the more subtle issues related to the effects of moisture and proper control continues to evolve. As a result, while effective moisture control ultimately rests on scientific principles, it also must be implemented by home builders and contractors who bring a more practical approach to the construction process.

To understand how to inspect for moisture intrusion, property inspectors must understand moisture control in relation to building standards and construction practices, and the successful implementation of these standards and practices. The topics in this book have been designed to combine the most common building standards for controlling moisture with the practice of property inspection.

Introduction

This book is designed primarily for residential and commercial property inspectors. It will help the inspector learn how to inspect for moisture intrusion in buildings, structures and homes. The student-inspector will learn about the specific details and areas of a building to explore and potentially discover defects that may cause moisture-related problems. The inspector will learn about the design, construction and maintenance of houses that help manage moisture effectively.

This publication instructs the inspector in the best building practices and standards that make a home moisture-resistant. Building methods and construction techniques are essential for an inspector to understand. Building components that are defective, incorrectly installed, or simply missing can produce moisture-related problems. Moisture intrusion into a building can cause major structural damage and can threaten the safety of its occupants. When an inspector knows what a properly installed building component looks like, then recognizing an installation defect is easy. Education and training on the best and latest building practices for controlling moisture are essential for every property inspector.

One of the main duties of an inspector is to identify and report on building components that, due to improper installation or poor condition, may cause moisture intrusion. By studying moisture-resistant building practices and standards, a variety of the most common moisture-related problems in homes can be inspected for, found, confirmed, diagnosed, explained and documented during an inspection.

Moisture-related problems include rain penetration, structural decay, mold growth, high indoor humidity, condensation, a wet foundation, ice dams, and many other issues that are familiar to builders, homeowners and insurers. For the most part, these problems are preventable and manageable. While Benjamin Franklin's advice that "an ounce of prevention is worth a pound of cure" was originally focused on preventing fires, it applies equally well to preventing moisture problems in homes.

Drawing from practical experience and the latest available technical resources, this manual assembles proven best practices for moisture management. These practices address topics directly related to moisture control, such as window flashing, as well as less obvious issues that also influence the behavior of water in a house, such as the implications of duct leakage. The application of these practices can provide a home with multiple lines of defense against moisture, the result being that, as a home ages and as certain details and components begin to fail, the overall structure will still manage moisture effectively.

Also, many of the best practices featured in this guide are tailored for important site-specific factors, such as climate and decay hazards, that may vary widely around the U.S. The absence of these best building practices in a home's construction should be reported and communicated by the inspector to his or her client.

Effective moisture management involves a degree of uncertainty. The best practices for moisture management should not be construed as absolutes. Equally effective or better alternatives are possible and may be discovered during an inspection. The absence of a particular building component discovered during an inspection may not necessarily mean that moisture problems exist at the property.

Part 1: Scope and Approach

The scope of this book is focused on relatively common moisture issues encountered in one- and two-family dwellings, both attached and detached. The best practices for moisture management featured here are intended to address the issues in typical light-frame wood construction using common building systems. The practices deal with direct moisture issues, as well as related design concerns that also influence moisture management in a house.

Many of these best practices will be found during a typical home inspection. The lack of a particular best practice for moisture management may not necessarily be a construction defect potentially leading to moisture intrusion. Caution during an inspection is advised when inspecting for construction practices because a typical home inspection is strictly non-invasive and visual-only. Building components related to moisture management will usually be hidden, covered or restricted in some way in a visual-only building inspection.

Home inspectors are not typically expected to determine a component's conformance with the manufacturer's installation recommendations, or a component's or system's compliance with local building codes and regulations.

Given the diversity of housing materials and construction styles in the U.S., the general approach advised is to present moisture-management strategies that can lead to several viable solutions, rather than specifying a single solution that assumes the use of a limited selection of materials and details. In sections where a single detail is provided, additional details and variations may also provide workable solutions. This approach gives the inspector a wide range of installation techniques and materials to look for and discuss with the client. Discovering different materials and applications may reflect the owner's, builder's and/or contractor's material choices, design preferences, and strategies for meeting various local code requirements.

Moisture Movement

Understanding Moisture Movement

To be able to inspect for moisture intrusion and related problems, an inspector should understand the basics of how moisture can move through a house.

Moisture and water vapor move in and out of a house in three ways:

- with air currents;
- by diffusion through materials; and
- by heat transfer.

Of these three, air movement accounts for more than 98% of all water vapor movement in building cavities. Air naturally moves from a high-pressure area to a lower one by the easiest path possible — generally, through any available hole or crack in the building envelope. Moisture transfer by air currents is very fast — in the range of several hundred cubic feet of air per minute. Thus, to control air movement, a house should have any unintended air paths thoroughly and permanently sealed.

The other two driving forces — diffusion through materials, and heat transfer — are much slower processes. Most common building materials slow moisture diffusion to a large degree, although they never stop it completely. Insulation also helps reduce heat transfer or flow.

The laws of physics govern how moist air reacts within various temperature conditions. The study of the properties of moist air is technically referred to as psychrometrics. A psychrometric chart is used by professionals to determine at what temperature and moisture concentration water vapor begins to condense. This is called the dew point. By learning how to determine the dew point, you will better understand how to diagnose moisture problems in a house.

Relative humidity (RH) refers to the amount of moisture contained in a quantity of air compared to the maximum amount of moisture the air could hold at the same temperature. As air warms, its ability to hold water vapor increases; this capacity decreases as air cools.

For example, according to the psychrometric chart, air at 68° F (20° C) with 0.216 ounces of water (H_2O) per pound of air (14.8g H_2O/kg air) has 100% RH. The same air at 59° F (15° C) reaches 100% RH with only 0.156 ounces of water per pound of air (10.7g H_2O/kg air). The colder air holds about 28% less moisture than the warmer air does. The moisture that the air can no longer hold condenses on the first cold surface it encounters — the dew point. If this surface is within an exterior wall cavity, the result will be wet insulation and framing.

In addition to air movement, one can also control temperature and moisture content. Since insulation reduces heat transfer (or flow), it also moderates the effect of temperature across the building envelope cavity. In most U.S. climates, properly installed vapor diffusion-retarders can be used to reduce the amount of moisture transfer. Except in deliberately ventilated spaces, such as attics, insulation and vapor diffusion-retarders work together to reduce the opportunity for condensation to form in a house's ceilings, walls and floors.

Part 2: Inspecting for Moisture Intrusion

General

This section covers building installation methods and recommendations for each major building system. For example, if a foundation cross-section and related plan notes are being reviewed for moisture performance, useful best-practice information can be found in the "Foundations" section within the discussions of design considerations, such as "Basement Wall Insulating and Finishing." Thus, particular parts of a plan can be quickly reviewed and red-lined to include moisture-related best practices. Issues concerning moisture vapor tend to overlap building systems and, as such, they are discussed in individual sections (such as those regarding walls), as well as in a comprehensive section that deals with the systems' interactions of vapor-related problems.

Inspectors and Codes

The following sections refer to building practices that prevent moisture problems that may be consistent with minimum building codes and standards. There are practices that go beyond the code requirements. Home inspectors are typically not required to inspect for code compliance. However, knowledge and an understanding of building codes and standards are sometimes necessary in order to inspect for building practices that are causing moisture-related problems, such as missing kickout flashing that should be installed according to model U.S. building standards. Commenting upon codes and standards is beyond the scope of a typical home inspection. Home inspectors are not code inspectors, but home inspectors do use building codes and standards as reference sources.

Moisture-Resistant Roof Systems

Inspecting and Identifying Roof Coverings for Typical Sloped Roofs

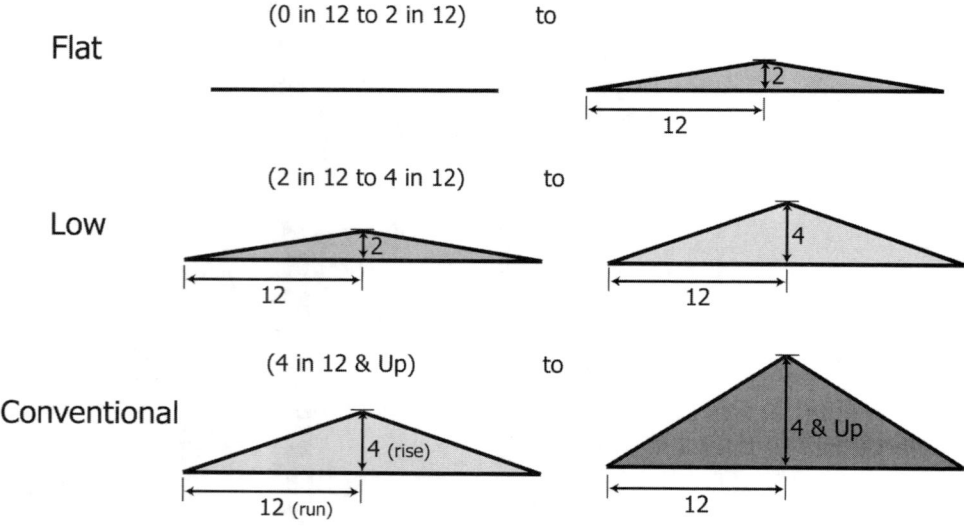

The roof covering materials provide the home's first line of defense against the elements. They also tend to be the most exposed components of a building's exterior envelope. Therefore, roof coverings should be selected, detailed and installed to provide durable resistance to water penetration. Because more than 75% of all homes in the U.S. use composition roof shingles, the focus of this section is on this type of roof covering.

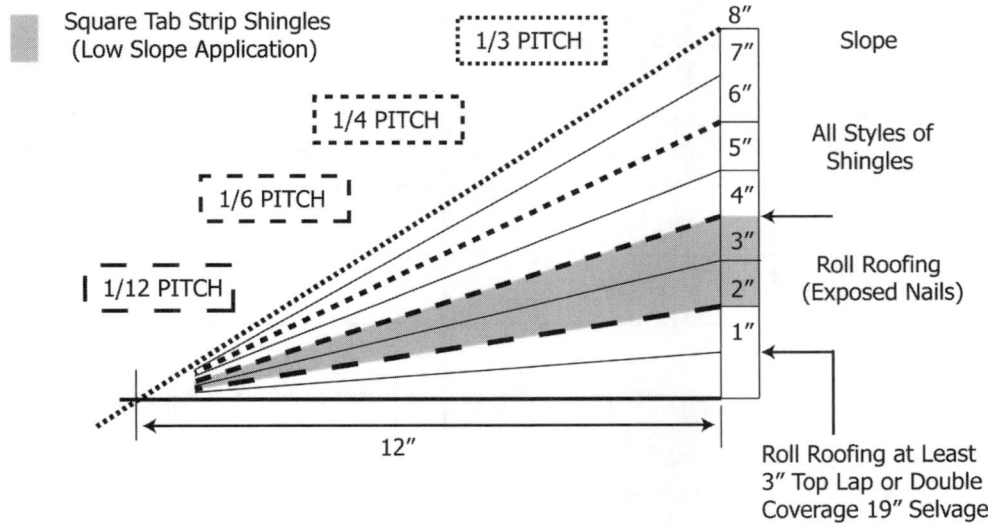

This design consideration deals with selecting and using a reasonably durable and weather-resistant roof covering. These considerations are intended to enhance or help fulfill the objectives for a roof installation as found in the 2006 International Residential Code (IRC), which states:

> *R903.1 General. Roof decks shall be covered with approved roof coverings secured to the building or structure... Roof assemblies shall be designed and installed in accordance with this code and the approved manufacturer's installation instructions such that the roof assembly shall serve to protect the building or structure.*

Building codes don't address many of the details required for a complete and proper installation of the many available roofing products. Therefore, the statement regarding "in accordance with... manufacturer's installation instructions" should not be taken lightly. Industry-standard installation guidelines are also important resources. Home inspectors are not usually expected to determine conformance with the manufacturer's installation recommendations, or compliance with local building codes and regulations. However, there are many standards and building practices that could be checked during a typical home inspection. For example, most (if not all) asphalt-composition shingle manufacturers will void the warranty if shingles are installed on a sloped roof with a pitch of less than 2:12.

Home inspectors should know the importance of the minimum roof slopes for the various roof coverings. Underlayment installations are not readily visible for existing homes but can be inspected during construction. Life expectancies are also valuable information for an inspector to know and refer to.

Table 1 - Roof Covering Selection Data			
Roof Covering Types	Minimum Roof Pitch[a]	Weight[b] (lbs per sf)	Service Life[c] (yrs)
Composition Shingle	2:12	2 to 4	15 to 30
Wood Shingle	3:12	3 to 4	15 to 30
Metal (standing seam)	1/4:12	1 to 3	20 to 50+
Concrete/Clay Tile	2-1/2:12	9 to 25	50+
Slate	4:12	9+	50 to 100
Built-Up Roof	1/4:12	6	12 to 30
Synthetic Membrane	1/4:12	1	20+

a. A minimum roof pitch of 4:12 is allowable with normal use of single-layer roofing underlayment. However, a minimum 2:12 roof pitch is permissible for composition shingles, provided that 15# tarred felt underlayment is doubled and cemented together.

b. Weights are approximate; refer to manufacture date.

c. Service life may vary widely from these estimates due to differences in local climate, installation practice, and conditions at the time of installation, product variations, maintenance history, and other factors. Estimates are based upon Life Expectancy of Housing Components, NAHB, 2007.

Inspecting Roof Pitch and Material Properties

While the selection of a roof covering is primarily driven first by cost, local custom and aesthetics, there are other factors that go into this decision. These include roof pitch, weight, service life, and special-use conditions. Table 1 above and the following discussion compare these factors for different roof coverings as they relate to water-shedding and water-resistant roof coverings.

Understand Minimum Roof Pitch and Check Underlayment

Steep-slope roof systems are defined by the National Roofing Contractors Association (NRCA) as systems designed for installation on slopes greater than 3:12 (14 degrees). Steep-slope roofs are water-shedding, not waterproof. Therefore, roof pitch is limited in accordance with Table 1 for various steep-slope roofing products. To prevent water leaks, these roof systems rely on fast drainage, adequate overlapping of elements, and use of underlayment as a backup layer of protection. For composition shingles and concrete and clay tiles, the following image shows a double underlayment detail to be used on slopes of less than 4:12 for these two roof coverings. For composition shingles and concrete and clay tiles, it shows a double underlayment detail to be used on slopes of less than 4:12 for these two roof coverings (see Table 1, Note a).

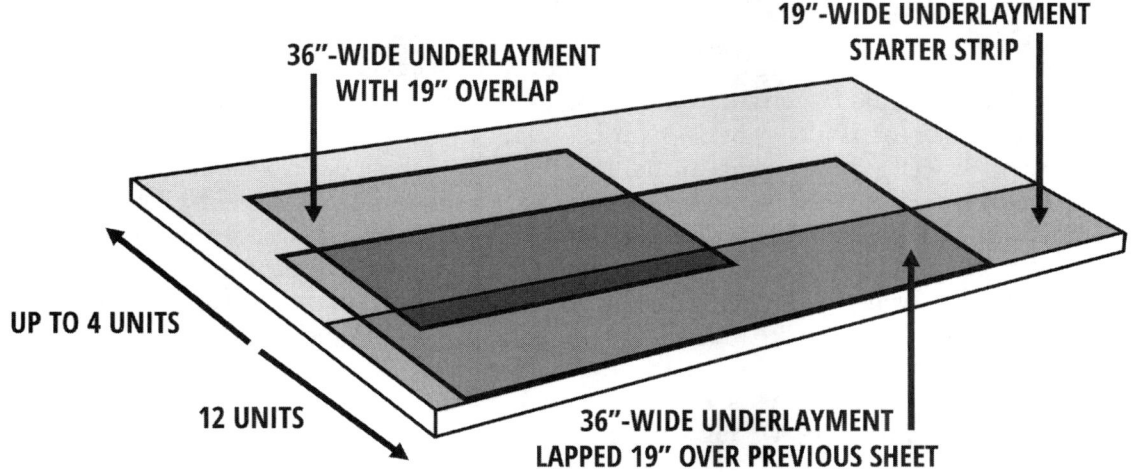

For roof slopes between 2:12 (two units vertical in 12 units horizontal = a 9.5-degree slope) to 4:12 (four units vertical in 12 units horizontal = a 18.5-degree slope), underlayment should be two layers applied in the following manner:

- A 19-inch strip of underlayment felt should be applied parallel to and starting at the eaves, and fastened sufficiently to hold in place. Starting at the eaves, 36-inch-wide sheets of underlayment should be applied, overlapping successive sheets at 19 inches, and fastened sufficiently to hold in place.

For roof slopes of 4:12 and greater:

- One layer of underlayment should be applied in shingle-like fashion. It should start from the eaves and run parallel to the eaves. It should overlap 2 inches. It should be fastened sufficiently to hold in place. End-laps of the underlayment should be offset by at least 6 feet.

In areas where there is a history of ice forming along the eaves and causing a backup of water, an ice barrier that consists of at least two layers of underlayment cemented together, or of a self-adhering polymer-modified bitumen sheet, shall be used in lieu of normal underlayment, and extend from the lowest edges of all roof surfaces to a point at least 24 inches inside the exterior wall line of the building. Detached structures without conditioned areas are the exception.

By contrast, low-slope systems are designed as waterproof roof systems and use roof coverings designed for pitches as low as 1/4:12. While low-slope roofs are commonly known as flat roofs, an actual flat roof surface is a design mistake. There should always be some slope.

Inspectors should report a flat roof that is actually flat as being defective.

Optimal Slope of a Water-Shedding Roof

Considering several factors, a moderate roof pitch (e.g., 4:12 to 7:12) provides a favorable balance of pros and cons for water-shedding roof systems. For example, lower roof pitches will tend to decrease drainage efficiency, allow debris to accumulate, and increase wind uplift loads on the roof. In addition, as the roof ages or becomes damaged, leaks are likely to be more severe. While very steep roof pitches will tend to increase drainage efficiency, they increase the building and roof's exposure to lateral wind loads. Furthermore, water flow velocity will be increased (particularly at valleys) that may cause scour, accelerated wear, and over-shooting of gutters. Also, very steep roofs are more difficult and less safe to access for construction, maintenance and replacement. An attic designed for usable space will also introduce other considerations related to roof slope.

Considerations for Low-Slope Roofs & Special Applications

Low-slope and special roof-covering applications require special attention to material selection. When in doubt, help should be sought from roofing experts or the manufacturer. For example, a waterproof membrane for a balcony or deck surface should be installed. The surface will need to be wear-resistant as well as waterproof. In addition, the surface must drain a minimum of 1/4:12 toward the balcony or deck perimeter or internal drains. Flashing must be carefully detailed at intersections with building walls and membrane penetrations. In addition, some low-slope roof applications may require special drainage features, such as drain inlets, scuppers, and emergency overflow outlets, to prevent ponding of water due to extreme rainfall events or sagging of roof members due to snow load. Beware that many of these design requirements may be found in the commercial building plumbing code rather than the residential building code. As a result of these design and installation considerations, some membrane roofing manufacturers require their products to be installed by their own network of certified installers.

What's the Weight?

Although the weight of the roof covering it is not directly related to a moisture-management concern, it is a consideration when inspecting the structure of the roof. Most homes are designed for a maximum roof-covering weight of no more than 5 psf (pounds per square foot). When replacing the roof on an existing home, a structural analysis should be performed if a light roof covering is being replaced by a much heavier roof covering.

Estimating Service Life

The service life estimates in Table 1 are rough approximations designed to inform the inspector about various roof coverings. For a more thorough estimate of service life considerations, the inspector should refer to a web-based, automated assessment tool known as the "Durability Doctor." This tool was created by the National Institute for Standards and Technology (NIST) under HUD's Partnership for Advancing Technology in Housing (PATH) Program, and is hosted on the PATH website at **www.pathnet.org**.

Wind-Resistant Roofing in High-Wind Areas

When specified and installed properly, many roofing systems will provide adequate performance in high-wind regions. However, there are a few items deserving special attention.

Wrappers with Wind Ratings

This product should be rated for the local wind speed. For example, in areas subject to hurricane-force winds, the wrappers of asphalt composition shingles should be labeled as meeting the ASTM D 3161-Class F test for wind speeds of 110 mph and higher.

During a typical home inspection on an existing home, this type of identification will not be possible. However, on a new home being built, or on a roof installation project, the rating identification could be accomplished.

There Is Good and Bad Fastening

The manufacturer's installation instructions should be followed, and the fasteners should be properly installed (e.g., appropriate fastener spacing, fasteners installed without damaging material, etc.). In general, six roofing nails per shingle, rather than the standard four nails, are required for composition shingles in high-wind regions. The roofing fasteners should not be over-driven (so that the head damages or tears the shingle) to avoid complete loss of shingle strips, which is a major cause of extensive water damage to the contents of homes during wind-driven rain events. Attention to fastening quality is equally important for other roofing materials, such as tile and metal.

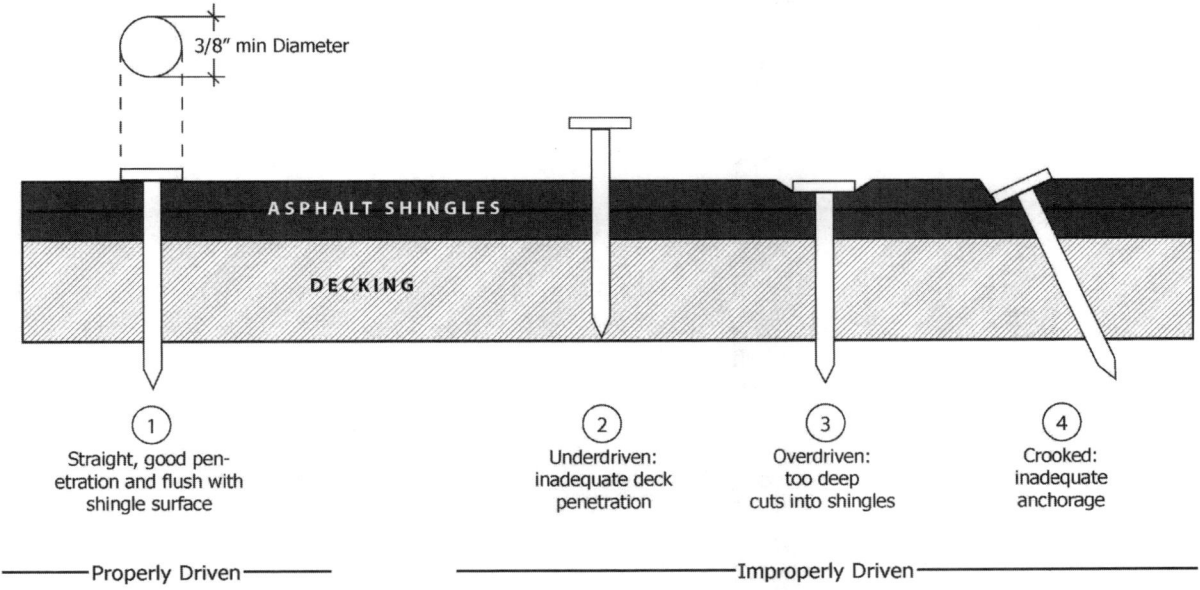

Underlayment

Typical 15# tarred felt underlayment provides backup protection against water intrusion only as long as the primary roofing material remains intact. It is not intended for direct exposure in the event of loss of the primary roofing system in a severe wind-driven rain event. To enhance protection against water intrusion and damage to the building and contents in severe wind-driven rain climates, a roofing contractor should apply a continuous strip of bituminous adhesive tape to sheathing joints prior to installing the underlayment. This practice provides a level of protection against water intrusion, even in the event of severe wind damage to the primary roofing. For further backup protection, a self-adhering bituminous membrane may be applied to the entire roof.

Flashing

Longer-than-normal flashing overlaps and vertical legs could be installed in anticipation of severe wind-driven rain and wind pressure. Roof-edge flashing should be securely attached to the substrate.

Check the Roof Sheathing

The roof covering is only as strong as the substrate to which it is attached. During an inspection of a new roof, before the underlayment and other roofing materials are installed, be sure to inspect for proper installation of the roof sheathing. Because underlayment is sometimes installed by the framing contractor immediately after completion of the roof sheathing installation, a timely inspection is critical. Roof sheathing in high-wind areas should be attached with minimum 8d (0.113-inch diameter) deformed shank nails, or 8d common nails (0.131-inch diameter) spaced 6 inches on-center at all framing members. Full round-head or D-head nails should be specified and should not be over-driven into or through the sheathing, as this severely weakens the connection.

Roofing and Re-Roofing for Hail Damage Protection

Composition shingles rated for hail resistance or other more resistant roofing products should be installed for protection from hail damage. Since hail can occur in so many parts of the country at least occasionally, the greater the likelihood of hail, the more often enhanced shingles should be seen at inspections. The map shown below is presented as an example, and illustrates the mean number of days per year for a hail event that is damaging and/or has hail of 2 inches in diameter. When available, maps and indexes found in building codes should be referenced.

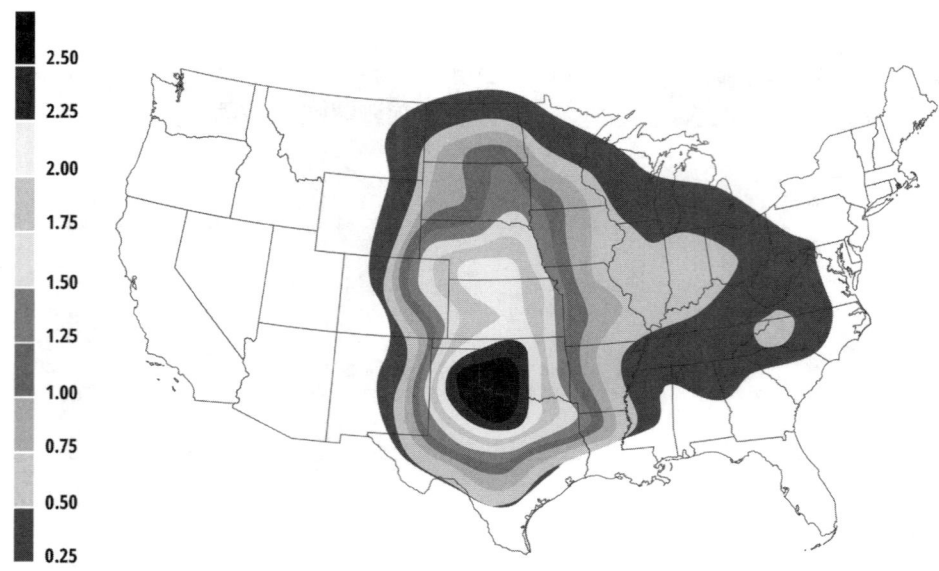

Probability (%) of 2-inch Hail Day on 960506/0000 (1980-1994)

Composition shingles tested in accordance with UL 2218 and rated as Class 4 may be used for improved hail resistance. (Classes range from a low of 1 to a high of 4.) In some states, such as Texas, hail damage insurance premiums may be reduced with the use of impact-resistant roofing. In fact, in October 2004, the Texas Department of Insurance provided an online listing of manufacturers of products that meet the state's roofing discount requirements.

Another consideration for protecting roofs from hail damage involves re-roofing. Re-roofing over an existing layer of composition shingles, while generally permitted by code, reduces the ability of the newer shingles to resist impact damage from hail. Therefore, in hail-prone regions, the insurance industry recommends (and local code may require) that re-roofing should include removal of the existing layer(s) of old composition-shingle roofing.

Checking for Concentrated and Obstructed Roof Drainage

In modern construction, adding complexity to roof plans is commonly done to improve curb appeal. But adding complexity to the roof drainage system can also create long-term moisture problems. A balance is needed so that roof rainwater flows aren't excessively concentrated or obstructed, as shown at right. If these conditions cannot be avoided, then affected regions of the roof should be adequately detailed and waterproofed, and guttering should be appropriately designed to channel water off the roof and away from the building. These are critical areas to inspect.

Minimal Roof Penetrations

Roof penetrations increase the likelihood of water leaks due to failed gaskets, sealants and flashing. The number of roof penetrations may be reduced by a variety of technologies and strategies, including:

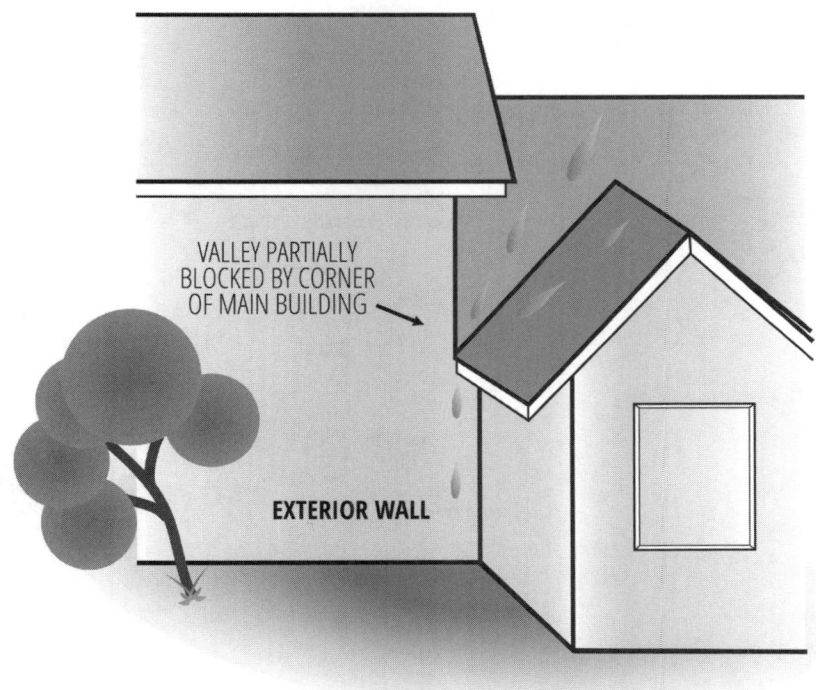

- air-admittance valves (AAVs) to reduce or eliminate plumbing vent-stack penetrations;

- consolidation of vent stacks below the roof;

- exhaust fan caps routed through walls instead of through the roof;

- high-efficiency combustion appliances, which can be sidewall-vented; and

- electrically powered HVAC equipment and hot water heaters that do not require flue pipes.

The more penetrations an inspector finds passing through the roof covering, the greater the potential for moisture intrusion.

Roof Flashing

Water penetration is commonly associated with flashing and detailing problems around roof penetrations, eaves, and wall intersections with a lower roof section. The following best practices describe flashing details for common applications in residential construction that inspectors should be able to recognize. These conceptual details are intended to help the inspector understand the objective for roof flashing, as found in the 2006 IRC:

> R903.2 Flashing. Flashings shall be installed in such a manner so as to prevent moisture from entering the wall and roof through joints in copings, through moisture-permeable materials, and at intersections with parapet walls and other penetrations through the roof plane.

Building codes in the U.S. provide only basic performance concepts for use and detailing of flashing. Therefore, it is imperative that designers and builders consider the issue of roof flashing as a key element of construction plan detailing, construction trade coordination, and field quality-control. Oftentimes, inspectors discover flashing details incorrectly installed, or even flashing that is missing. Manufacturers' recommendations and the industry's standard installation guidelines provide a valuable resource for inspectors to understand flashing details.

Flashing Details for Roofs

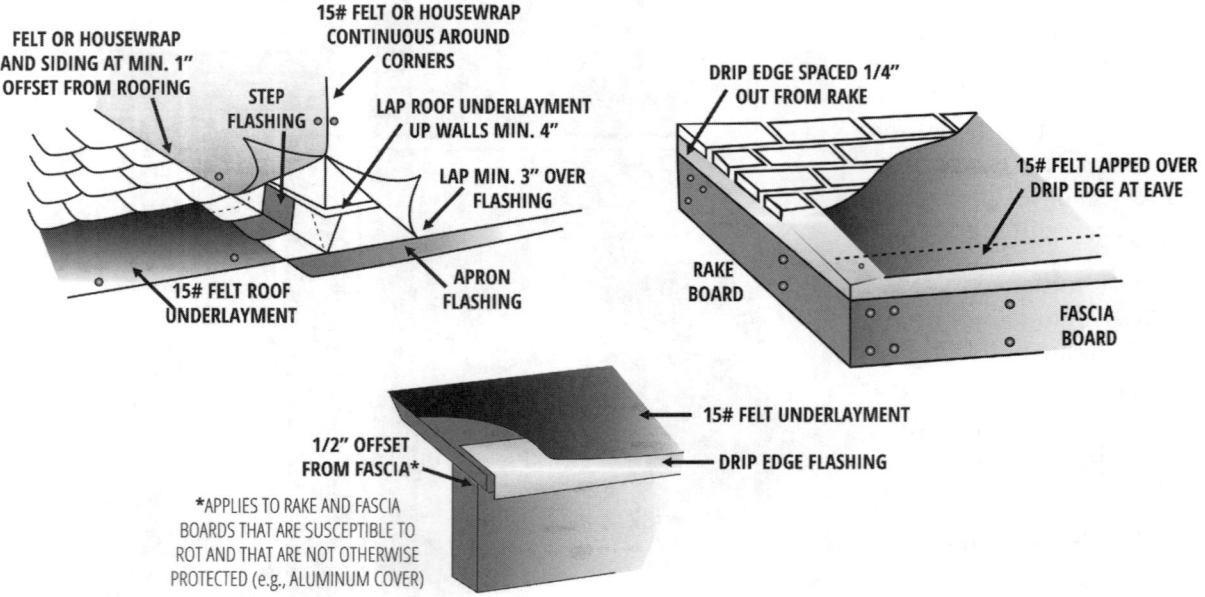

The images above and on the following two pages provide models for correct flashing installation techniques for asphalt composition shingle roofing, which is the most common roofing material used in residential construction in the U.S. For flashing details for other roofing types, the inspector should refer to the manufacturer's literature and industry guidelines.

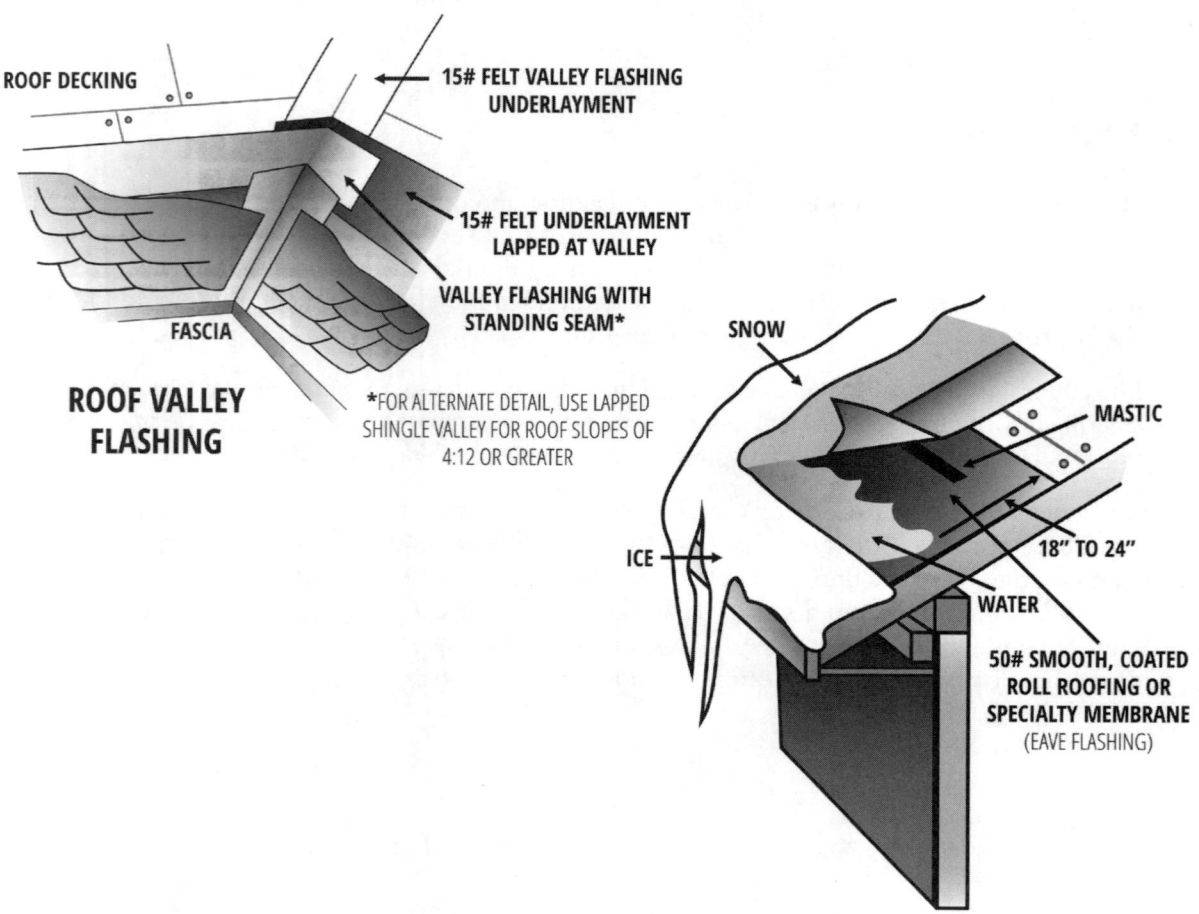

To avoid roof leaks, appropriate flashing details should be installed wherever possible; roofing cement and caulk should not be solely relied upon for adequate sealing purposes. In addition, improper or missing kick-out flashing (which may involve only a single roof flashing component) is associated with some of the more severe cases of localized moisture damage to walls. This flashing element is highlighted in the graphic on the following page. It is commonly referred to as a kick-out (or kickout) flashing or an end-dam flashing.

To ensure that the ice-dam flashing at the eaves extends 24 inches horizontally beyond the exterior wall, the slope of the roof should be accounted for.

Table 2 offers nominal width requirements for the ice-dam flashing at the eaves based on different roof slopes and the eaves' overhangs. Note that for many scenarios, a single 36-inch roll of flashing may not be sufficient.

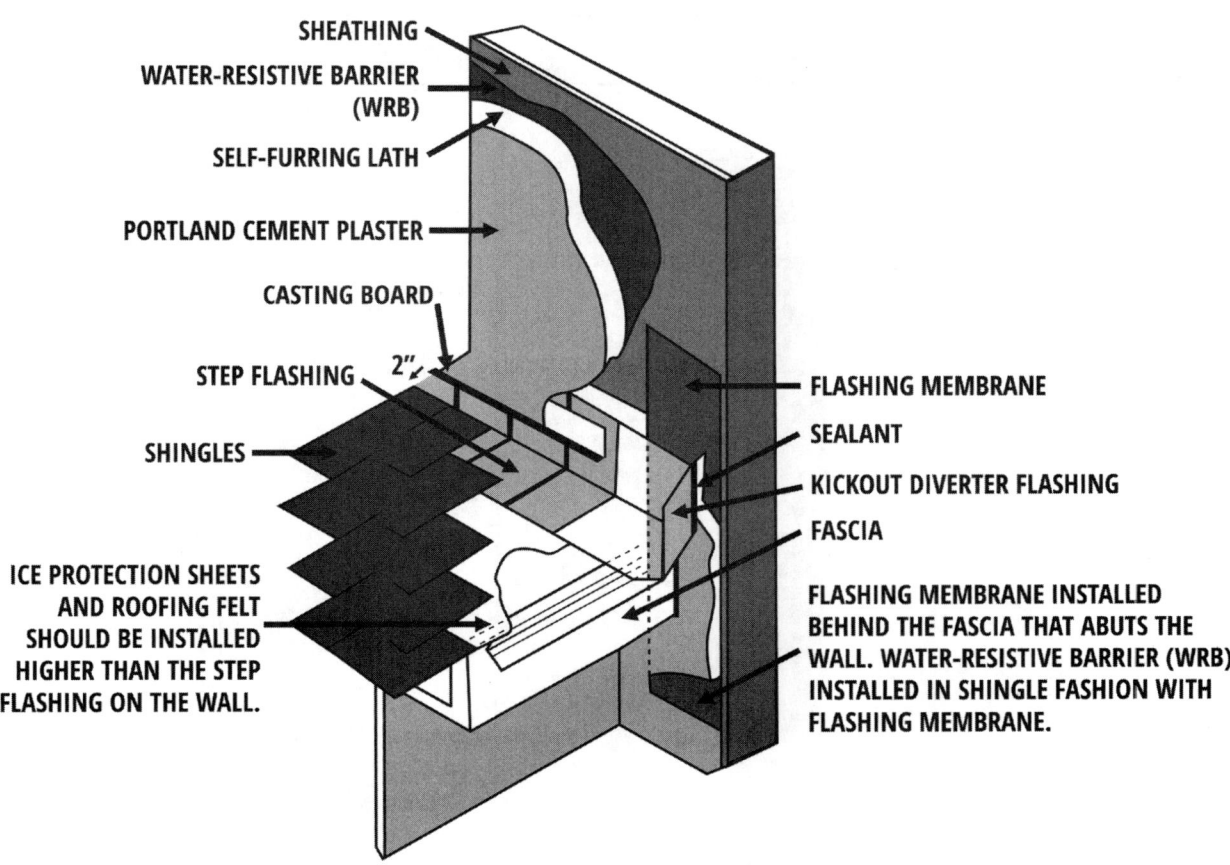

Table 2 - Eave Ice Dam Flashing Width (inches)						
Eave Overhang (inches)	Roof Slope					
	4:12	5:12	6:12	7:12	8:12	9:12
8	34	35	36	37	38	40
12	38	39	40	42	43	45
16	42	43	45	46	48	50
24	51	52	54	56	58	60

Quiz #1

1. Moisture and water vapor move in and out of a house in three ways: with air currents; by diffusion through materials; and by _____ transfer.

☐ heat

☐ water

☐ cold

2. Of the three main ways that moisture moves through a house, _____ movement accounts for more than 98% of all water vapor movement in building cavities.

☐ air

☐ vertical

☐ gravitational

3. _____ refers to the amount of moisture contained in a quantity of air compared to the maximum amount of moisture the air could hold at the same temperature.

☐ Moisture content (MC)

☐ Relative humidity (RH)

☐ Relativity transfer (RT)

4. T/F: Roof coverings provide the first line of defense against the elements and tend to be the most exposed components of a building's exterior envelope.

☐ True

☐ False

5. The minimum pitch for a composition-shingle roof is _____.

☐ 8:12

☐ 6:12

☐ 2:12

6. For roof slopes of 2:12 to 4:12, there should be _____ layers of underlayment applied.

☐ four

☐ three

☐ two

7. Re-roofing over an existing layer of composition shingles, while generally permitted by code, reduces the ability of the newer shingles to resist impact damage from _____.

☐ hail

☐ UV rays

☐ water

8. T/F: Roofing cement and caulk are adequate substitutes for general flashing details in order to prevent roof leaks.

     ☐ True
     ☐ False

Answer Key is on page 115.

Roof Ventilation and Insulation

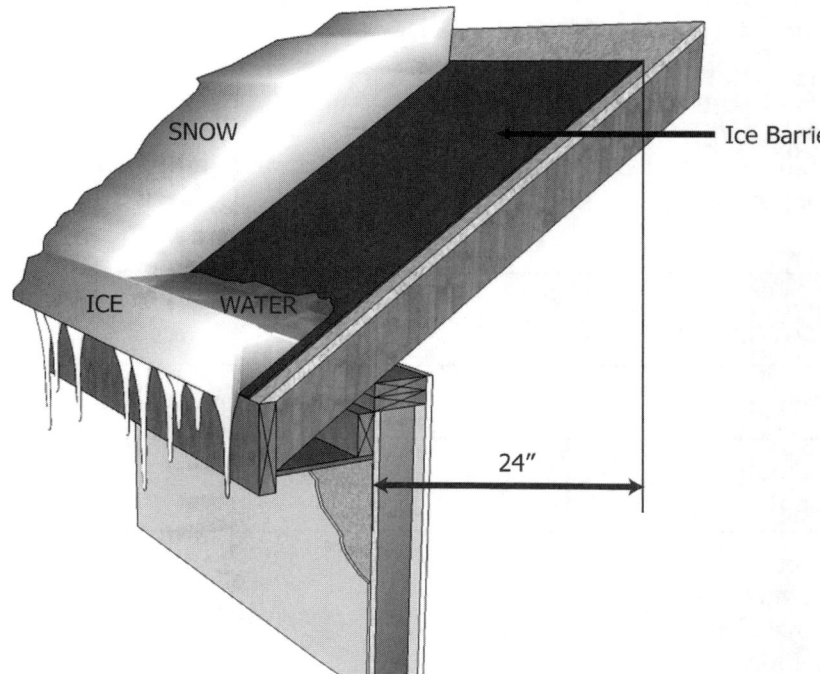

Roof system ventilation and insulation are important for a number of reasons, including:

- condensation control;
- temperature control;
- energy efficiency; and
- the prevention of chronic ice dam formation.

Ventilation of attic areas is intended to prevent the accumulation of moisture vapor in the attic/roof space and to dry low levels of condensation that may form on the underside of a roof deck. Ventilation is also intended to reduce the temperature of the roof deck during hot weather to improve shingle durability.

Reducing the attic's temperature through ventilation and insulation also improves energy efficiency during hot periods. And in the case of ice dams, elevated attic and roof temperature during the winter can cause snow on the roof to melt. Insulation and roof ventilation help to keep the roof's exterior surface cold and help minimize the development of melted water and, consequently, ice dams.

Ventilating roofs in hot and humid conditions may add (rather than remove) moisture from attics and enclosed roof spaces. However, not ventilating roofs may void the asphalt-composition roofing manufacturer's warranty and slightly decrease the life expectancy of the roofing material due to increased temperature of the roof's surface.

Other tile, concrete and metal roofing materials would not be similarly affected. Employing an unvented attic space may require designing the attic/roof space as conditioned space, similar to that required when creating habitable space in the attic. There are several sources with more information on unvented attic designs. Traditional attic ventilation remains a cost-effective (though imperfect) solution for moisture control. In colder climates, roof ventilation serves to remove humidity and condensation from the roof/attic space and helps to prevent the chronic formation of ice dams at the eaves.

What Causes Ice Dams?

An ice dam is caused by the warming of an attic space. And while attic ventilation and insulation contribute to the prevention of ice dams by keeping attics cold, they can be overpowered by other attic warming effects—such as air leakage from the house into the attic through ceiling bypasses, chases, open gaps, or un-insulated ducts placed in the attic. If significant conditioned air escapes into the attic through bypasses, the attic ventilation will not be capable in preventing the warming of the roof decking and subsequent ice dams. Therefore, sealing air leaks between the house and the vented attic is essential to making attic ventilation work. See the section titled "Controlling Air Leakage" for information on inspecting for the methods/practices of preventing air leakage into attics. Air leakage from the interior into the attic also introduces moisture. If significant interior air leaks into an attic, attic ventilation may not be sufficient to prevent attic moisture and condensation problems.

Roof Ventilation Based on Climate and Insulation Amount

Attic spaces and roof cavities should be ventilated in accordance with minimum requirements of local building codes, as represented in Table 3.

Table 3 - Minimum Roof Ventilation Requirements	
Applicability Requirements	**Ventilation Amount[a]**
Vertical separation of inlet and outlet vents is less than 3 feet.	1:150
Vertical separation of inlet and outlet vents is at least 3 feet with balanced inlet and outlet vent areas[b], or a vapor retarder is installed on the warm side of the ceiling.	1:300
a. Values are given as a ratio of total net (unobstructed) open area of inlet plus outlet vents to total the horizontal projected area of the ventilated space. Therefore, vent size must be increased to account for obstructed vent area due to louvers and screens (refer to vent manufacturer technical data).	
b. Inlet and outlet vent areas shall be considered balanced, provided that at least 50% and not more than 80% of the required ventilating area is provided by ventilators located in the upper portion of the space to be vented.	

For enhanced protection against the formation of ice dams, Table 4 provides recommended levels of insulation and vent-area ratios as a function of the venting layout. These recommendations should be found in areas with a ground snow load greater than 30 pounds per square foot (psf), and in other areas where ice dams are a concern. The recommendations for ventilation in Table 4 can additionally be used by contractors to create multiple lines of defense for flashing to prevent ice dams at eaves. Also, the arrangement of vent areas must balance high (or outlet) and low (or inlet) vent openings.

Table 4 - Recommended Roof Ventilation Levels to Prevent Chronic Ice Dams (for climates with ground snow load ≥ 30 psf and other areas prone to ice dams)[ab]				
R-value of Roof/ Attic Insulation[c]	**Vertical Separation of Inlet (Eave/Cornice) and Outet (Ridge or Gable) Vents**			
	3 ft	6 ft	9 ft	12 ft
Vented Attic Roofs				
R-19	1:100	1:140	1:180	1:200
R-30	1:160	1:230	1:280	1:300

Table 4 - Recommended Roof Ventilation Levels to Prevent Chronic Ice Dams (for climates with ground snow load ≥ 30 psf and other areas prone to ice dams)[ab]				
R-38	1:200	1:290	1:300	1:300
R-49	1:260	1:300	1:300	1:300
Vented Cathedral Roofs				
R-19	1:100	1:140	1:250	1:250
R-30	1:160	1:230	1:250	1:250
R-38	1:200	1:250	1:250	1:250
R-49	1:250	1:250	1:250	1:250
Minimum Vent Depth for Air Passage in Cathedral Roofs				
Roof Pitch		Vent Depth[d]		
3:12 to 5:12		2"		
>5:12		1 to 1/2"		

a. This table applies to roofs with a pitch of at least 3:12, an R-value of at least R-19, and a distance between inlets and outlets of no more than 40 feet.

b. Values are given as a minimum ratio of total net open (unobstructed) area of inlet and outlet vents to total horizonal projected area of the ventilated space. Inlet and outlet areas shall be balanced to the minimum extent practicable. For example, on a simple gable roof, one-half of the calculated vent area shall be at the ridge and one-fourth at each of the two eaves.

c. For the purpose of determining ventilation requirements, roof/attic insulation shall meet or exceed insualtion amounts required by the local building code.

d. Minimum vent depths shall be maintained for the entire ventilation air flow path from eaves to ridge or gable vents.

Roof Overhangs and Projections

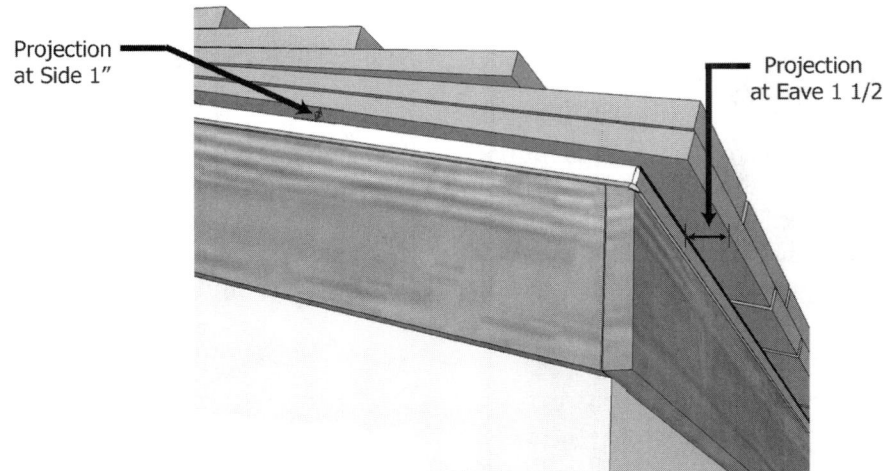

Projection at Side 1"

Projection at Eave 1 1/2"

Roof overhangs and projections, such as porch roofs and overhanging upper floors, provide the primary means to deflect rainwater away from building walls. Thus, the potential for water penetration through siding, windows and doors is minimized. Because the protection of roof overhangs increases with increasing overhang width, larger overhangs than those recommended in this section may be important in the consideration of weather-resistant wall-barrier design.

Roof overhangs offer limited benefit during periods of severe wind-driven rain conditions, such as thunderstorm fronts and tropical storms, and in arid regions where rain is not a major concern. In severe wind-driven rain climates, a well-performing weather-resistant barrier for walls is at least as important as providing roof overhangs. In high-wind areas, overhangs add wind-uplift load to the roof, and may require stronger roof-wall connections.

Table 5 - Recommended Minimum Roof Overhang Width[a]		
Decay Hazard Index	**Eave Overhang (inches)**	**Rake Overhang (inches)**
Less than 35	N/A	N/A
35 to 70	12	12
More than 70	24 or more	12 or more
a. Table based on typical two-story home with vinyl or similarly durable siding and eave gutters		

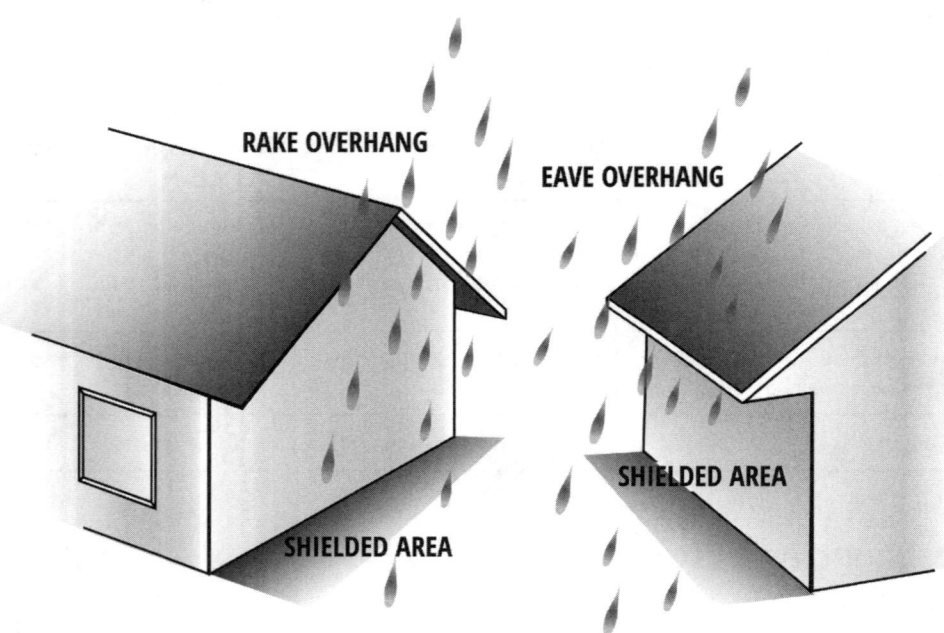

Roof Overhangs Should Be Based on Climate

Recommended minimum widths for roof overhangs for one- and two-story wood-frame buildings are shown in Table 5 and the image above. For taller structures, larger roof overhangs are desirable. Alternatively, porch roofs and upper-floor overhangs can be used to protect lower-story walls, in accordance with Table 5. A decay-hazard index map is provided on the next page to assist in using Table 5. It should be noted that some U.S. building codes do not regulate minimum widths for roof overhangs.

DECAY HAZARD INDEX

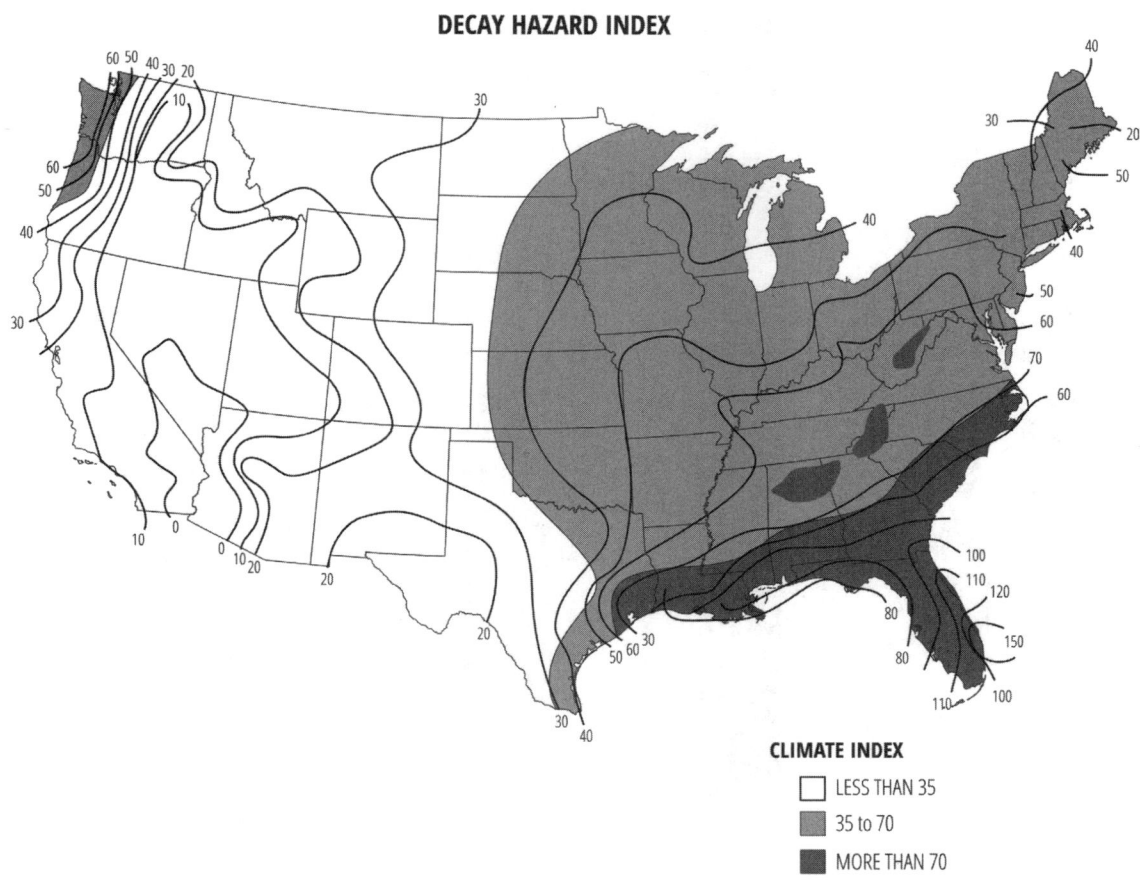

CLIMATE INDEX

☐ LESS THAN 35
▨ 35 to 70
■ MORE THAN 70

Roof Drainage, Gutters and Downspouts

While roof overhangs and porch roofs protect building walls from impinging rain, gutters serve to protect building walls and foundations from roof water runoff. Roof gutters, downspouts and leaders or diverters form the initial components of a drainage system for the building and site. A proper design of gutters and downspouts for water-shedding (steep-slope) roof systems should be looked for during an inspection.

Common problems with guttering are associated with installation and maintenance. Home inspectors can check if properly sized materials are being used, if guttering is appropriately sloped toward adequately sized downspouts, and if discharge is directed away from the building's foundation and perimeter. Discharging water at inside building corners should be avoided. Some local storm water codes may require special infiltration or filtration treatments of roof runoff.

Check Whether the Roof Drainage System Installed Is Properly Sized

Only two steps are required to properly design a steep-slope roof drainage system using standard guttering products.

STEP 1: Design Rainfall Intensity

The rainfall intensity for roof drainage design is sometimes based on a 10-year return period and five-minute duration (see map below). However, other design return periods and durations may be used effectively. Adjustment factors for other acceptable design conditions follow. A standardized design criterion in U.S. building codes does not exist, so practical experience and judgment are important.

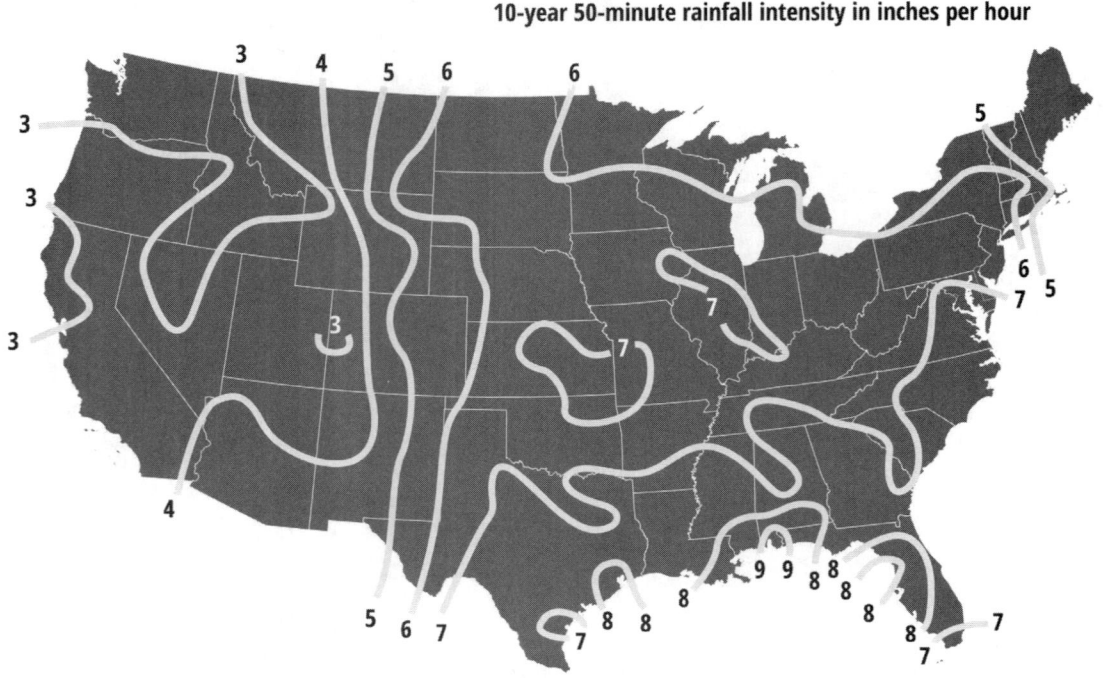

10-year 50-minute rainfall intensity in inches per hour

STEP 2: Roof Drainage System Spacing and Layout

Based on a selected gutter size and type, as well as the design rainfall intensity from Step 1, the maximum plan (horizontal) area of the roof that the gutter can adequately serve can be determined using Table 6. Based on this area and the roof's geometry, spacing and locations of downspouts can be determined, as shown in the following example. If using suggested sizes for downspouts, the gutter size will generally control the spacing of the downspouts. Downspouts with a dimension of less than 2 inches should be avoided. It is also generally recommended that downspouts should serve no more than 50 feet of gutter length. A commonly used gutter is the 5-inch K-style gutter with 2x3-inch rectangular downspouts.

Roof rainwater collected in gutters and delivered to grade via downspouts must then be moved away from the foundation onto properly graded soil using leaders and diverters. This third component is just as important as the first two, and should receive equal emphasis. Leaders should direct the downspout discharge a minimum of 2 feet away from the building perimeter. This can be done using splash blocks or an underground drainage pipe, such as corrugated polyethylene or smooth PVC piping, which discharges to a safe conveyance point. In particularly poor soil conditions, such as expansive clays or collapsible soil that has been severely weakened with increased moisture, the distance between the downspout discharge and the foundation should be increased.

| Table 6 - Maximum Allowable Tributary Roof Plan Area (roof slope ≤ 5:12) | | | | | | | | | |
| Gutter Size and Type | Design Rainfall Intensity (in/hr) | | | | | | | | Suggested Downspout |
	3	4	5	6	7	8	9	10	
5 1/2"-round	775	581	465	387	332	291	258	232	3"
6 1/2"-round	1272	954	763	636	545	477	424	382	3" or 4"
4" K-style	763	572	458	382	327	286	254	229	2x3
5" K-style	1399	1050	840	700	600	525	466	420	2x3 or 3x4
6" K-style	2279	1709	1367	1139	977	854	760	684	3x4

a. The tributary area served by gutters is defined by L x W. L is the length of the gutters to both sides of a downspout measured to termination of the gutter or to the high point (drainage divide) between downspouts. W is the plan (horizontal) distance from the eave to the ridge of the roof area served.

b. The values in the table assume gutters with a minimum slope to prevent ponding and reverse flow. For gutters sloped at 1/16 inch per foot or greater, the table values may be multiplied by 1.1.

c. Allowable drainage areas are intended for roof slopes ≤ 5:12. For steeper roof pitches, multiply the tabulated areas by 0.85.

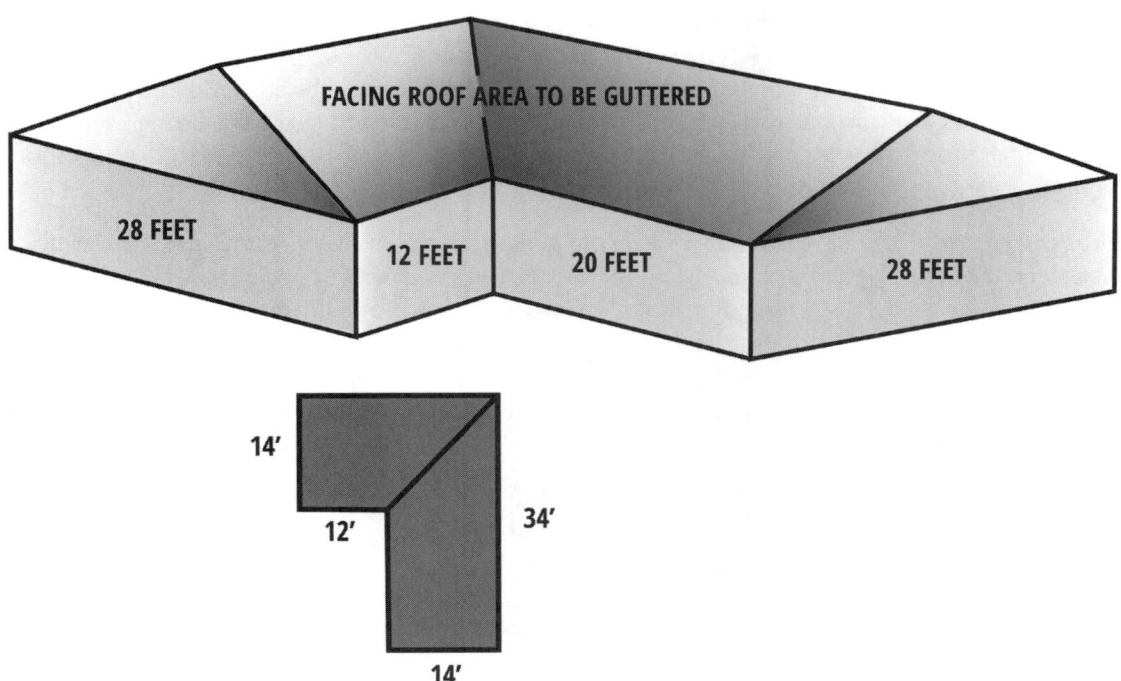

For the house model shown above, the following example is provided to illustrate this best practice:

STEP 1: From the map on the previous page, a design rainfall intensity of 7 inches per hour is determined for the site.

STEP 2: A 5-inch K-style gutter is selected from Table 6, with a maximum allowable roof tributary plan area of 600 feet².

Because the roof slope is 6:12 (Note c), the allowable tributary roof area is:

0.85 x 600 feet² = 510 feet².

The actual roof area for the side shown is:

14 x 34 feet + 14 x 12 feet = 644 feet².

The number of downspouts required is:

644 feet² ÷ 510 feet² = 1.3.

The number of downspouts should always be rounded up, so two downspouts should be used — one at each end of the L-shaped gutter layout. The downspout size may be 2x3 or 3x4, as suggested in Table 6.

Moisture-Resistant Wall Systems

What Is a Weather-Resistant Exterior Wall Envelope (WRE)?

This section discusses what a home inspector should look for with weather-resistant wall envelopes, which can include siding, water barriers, etc. Current U.S. building codes don't distinguish between the inherent performance differences of the various weather-resistant envelope (WRE) systems. In addition, selection of a siding system generally focuses on attributes such as appearance, cost and durability. There are different types of cladding systems that protect a building from rainwater penetration and its accumulation in walls. This section is intended to show the home inspector the basic installations of a weather-resistant wall envelope, as described in the 2006 International Residential Code:

> R703.1 General. Exterior walls shall provide the building with a weather-resistant exterior wall envelope. The exterior wall envelope shall include flashing as described in Section R703.8. The exterior wall envelope shall be designed and constructed in such a manner as to prevent the accumulation of water within the wall assembly by providing a water-resistant barrier behind the exterior veneer as required by Section R703.2 and a means of draining water that enters the assembly to the exterior. Protection against condensation in the exterior wall assembly shall be provided. There are some exceptions.

Due to the potential for water accumulation within the wall cavity, a water-resistant membrane must be installed behind any exterior siding and veneer. Under certain conditions, it is permissible to eliminate the membrane in detached accessory buildings, or where the siding, finish materials or lath provides the needed protection. The following 2006 IRC language defines a water-resistant barrier:

> R703.2 Water-resistive barrier. One layer of #15 asphalt felt or other approved water-resistive barrier shall be applied over the studs or sheathing of all exterior walls. Such felt or material shall be applied horizontally, with the upper layer lapped over the lower layer not less than 2 inches. Where joints occur, the felt shall be lapped at least 6 inches.

The installation of even the most weather-resistant wall envelope system on a house does not diminish the need for proper installation, particularly with regard to flashing details at penetrations. In addition, the use of roof overhangs provides performance benefits for all cladding systems by reducing the moisture load experienced over time, and by allowing greater opportunities for walls to dry in the event of periodic wetting due to wind-driven rain. The life expectancy of various siding materials may vary widely, from 10 to as long as 100 years or more, depending on type of material, climate exposure, maintenance, and other factors.

Understanding a Weather-Resistant Envelope System

A drained-cavity WRE system will provide fair to good protection in nearly all climates and building exposures, and should be considered as a common and broadly applied wall design for moisture protection. In more severe cases, such as climates with severe wind-driven rain or openly exposed buildings with no overhangs, and for wall designs involving different types of materials (e.g., conventional stucco), alternative WRE systems may be installed based on climate and building exposure. A three-step design process that accounts for these factors follows.

The drained-cavity system and other WRE approaches are illustrated and described below.

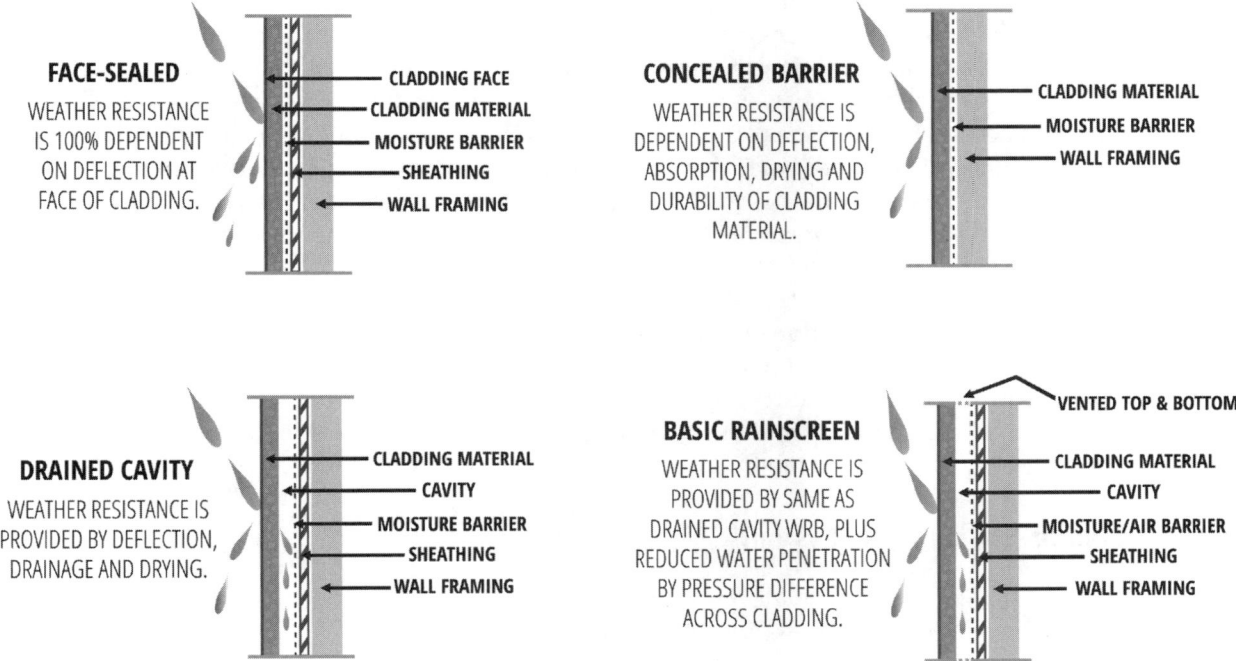

FACE-SEALED
WEATHER RESISTANCE IS 100% DEPENDENT ON DEFLECTION AT FACE OF CLADDING.
— CLADDING FACE
— CLADDING MATERIAL
— MOISTURE BARRIER
— SHEATHING
— WALL FRAMING

CONCEALED BARRIER
WEATHER RESISTANCE IS DEPENDENT ON DEFLECTION, ABSORPTION, DRYING AND DURABILITY OF CLADDING MATERIAL.
— CLADDING MATERIAL
— MOISTURE BARRIER
— WALL FRAMING

DRAINED CAVITY
WEATHER RESISTANCE IS PROVIDED BY DEFLECTION, DRAINAGE AND DRYING.
— CLADDING MATERIAL
— CAVITY
— MOISTURE BARRIER
— SHEATHING
— WALL FRAMING

BASIC RAINSCREEN
WEATHER RESISTANCE IS PROVIDED BY SAME AS DRAINED CAVITY WRB, PLUS REDUCED WATER PENETRATION BY PRESSURE DIFFERENCE ACROSS CLADDING.
VENTED TOP & BOTTOM
— CLADDING MATERIAL
— CAVITY
— MOISTURE/AIR BARRIER
— SHEATHING
— WALL FRAMING

Drained Cavity: A drained-cavity WRE relies on deflection, drainage and drying to protect the wall from moisture damage. There are many possible variations of this type of WRE. In general, a cavity exists to separate the cladding material from the surface of a moisture barrier placed on the structural wall behind the cladding. The depth of the cavity, however, may vary. For example, vinyl siding may be placed directly on the moisture barrier and still provide a cavity only restricted at points of contact (such as at nail flanges). A minimum cavity depth of 3/8- to 1/2-inch is sometimes recommended by use of vertical furring strips placed over the water barrier (drainage plane). Furring and flashing details around window and door openings must also be carefully installed. Drained cavities increase the life of exterior finishes on wood surfaces and promote drying of wall assemblies after wetting episodes. For brick veneer, a larger, 1-inch cavity depth is recommended to allow space for brick placement and mortar excesses.

Face-Sealed: This type of WRE relies exclusively on the ability of the outer surface of the wall and joints around penetrations to deflect water and prevent it from penetrating the wall surface. If a defect in the wall surface or joint detailing (such as caulk) exists or occurs over time, then water will penetrate and potentially accumulate in the wall, causing damage to any moisture-sensitive materials within the assembly. One example of this type of system is known as conventional or barrier EIFS (exterior insulation finish system). However, building standards only allow the use of a new type of drainable EIFS (i.e., drained cavity) on residential construction.

Concealed Barrier: This type of WRE relies on porous cladding material adhered to or placed directly on an internal (concealed) water barrier or drainage plane. A common example is conventional stucco applied on a layer of tarred felt paper attached to a wood-frame wall. This WRE system also relies primarily on deflection of rainwater, much like the face-sealed system, but also has a limited capability to absorb moisture to later dry and to drain moisture through weeps (weep screed) at the base of the wall. However, there is no open drainage pathway to allow water to freely drain from the concealed moisture barrier.

Specification and Installation of Drainage Planes (Moisture Barriers)

The secondary drainage plane (moisture barrier) is a key feature of any of the WRE systems that rely on drainage behind the exterior siding to improve moisture-resistant performance. Materials commonly used for this purpose include 15# tarred felt, various types of building wraps, and some water-resistant insulating sheathing products. It should be noted, however, that building wraps have varied levels of water resistance (as well as moisture-vapor permeability). The primary role of these materials is as a secondary drainage plane. In general, non-perforated building wraps tend to exhibit better water resistance than other types that may be perforated to allow for vapor permeability. In humid climates, moderate vapor permeability along with adequate water resistance may be preferable. Limited testing demonstrates that material candidates meeting these criteria include Tyvek®, R-Wrap®, and 15# felt. Because the secondary drainage plane is intended to drain moisture that penetrates siding and joints, its installation must be properly coordinated with flashing and other WRE components. In addition, all joints must be appropriately lapped (e.g., upper layer over top of lower layer). These features are hidden underneath the siding and must be properly installed prior to or in coordination with siding application. If water leaks behind the secondary drainage plane, it may cause more damage than if no drainage plane were present due to slower drying. Additional requirements when using building wraps as an exterior air barrier are discussed later.

Conversion of Existing WRE Systems

It is possible to adapt a drained-cavity approach to many traditional concealed barrier or face-sealed claddings, such as conventional Portland cement stucco and EIFS. Drainage EIFS products (a drained-cavity WRE) in lieu of barrier EIFS products (a face-sealed WRE) are the only types permitted for residential use under U.S. model building codes. Details to convert conventional Portland cement stucco (concealed barrier) to a drained-cavity system have been developed for use in British Columbia (Canada), where a high frequency of water intrusion problems has been experienced.

Rainscreen: A rainscreen can be considered an incremental improvement over the drained-cavity approach. This type of WRE is uncommon in the U.S. but has been used to some extent in Canada to address severe climate conditions. By the addition of some details to help reduce air-pressure differential across the cladding system during wind-driven rain events, water penetration into the drainage cavity is further limited. At a minimum, this approach involves use of an air barrier behind the cladding to resist wind pressures. Thus, wind pressure across the siding (which is vented and not airtight) is reduced and is less likely to result in water being driven through the siding due to pressure differentials across the siding. Also, the cavity between the cladding and water/air barrier must be compartmentalized by use of airtight blocking or furring at corners of the building, as a minimum practice. This feature prevents pressure differences on different surfaces of the building from "communicating" through a continuous cavity behind the cladding, which can cause unintended pressure differences across the cladding that drive rainwater through the cladding into the drainage cavity. Because many of the required components of a basic rainscreen system are already present in a simple drained-cavity wall system, drained-cavity systems are generally considered a more practical alternative for typical applications.

Drained-cavity WRE systems incorporate a wide range of cladding systems and may be considered a viable option for non-severe climates and building exposures.

The following is a three-step process for incorporating a WRE system on a house during construction.

STEP 1: Site Climate Conditions

Climatic conditions are categorized on the basis of the potential for wetting of walls, especially wetting from wind-driven rain. The exposure categories can be referred to as:

- severe: Severe climate conditions are conditions that result in frequent wetting due to wind-driven rain, such as coastal climates, and areas prone to frequent thunderstorm events;
- moderate: Moderate climate conditions pertain to those sites that are periodically exposed to wind-driven rain; and
- low: A low-climate condition is associated with relatively dry climates with little rainfall or wind-driven rain.

These classifications are intentionally subjective, as there are no clearly defined criteria in the U.S for assessing wind-driven rain and its effects on building wall systems. However, wind-driven rain climate data, as well as other related climate indices, may help guide the classification of a local climate based on these categories. Climate maps for this purpose are provided below and on the following page. The Decay Hazard Index Map shown previously may provide some additional guidance.

Wind Driven Rain (mm/yr)

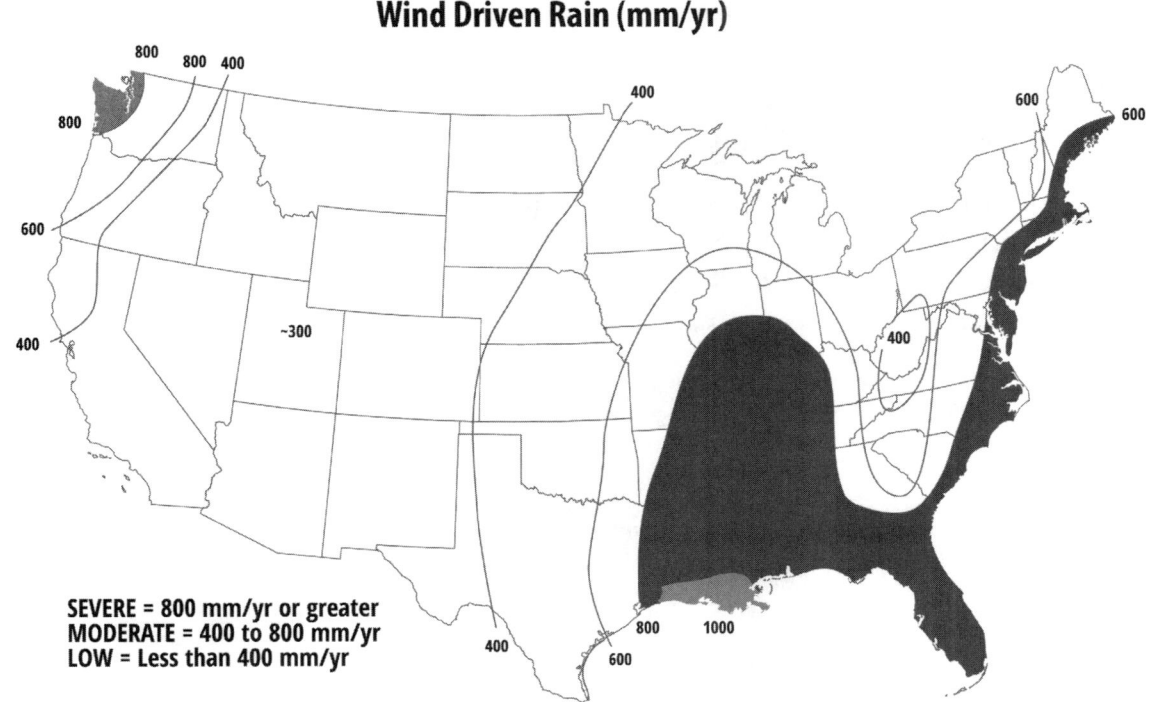

SEVERE = 800 mm/yr or greater
MODERATE = 400 to 800 mm/yr
LOW = Less than 400 mm/yr

MOISTURE INDEX

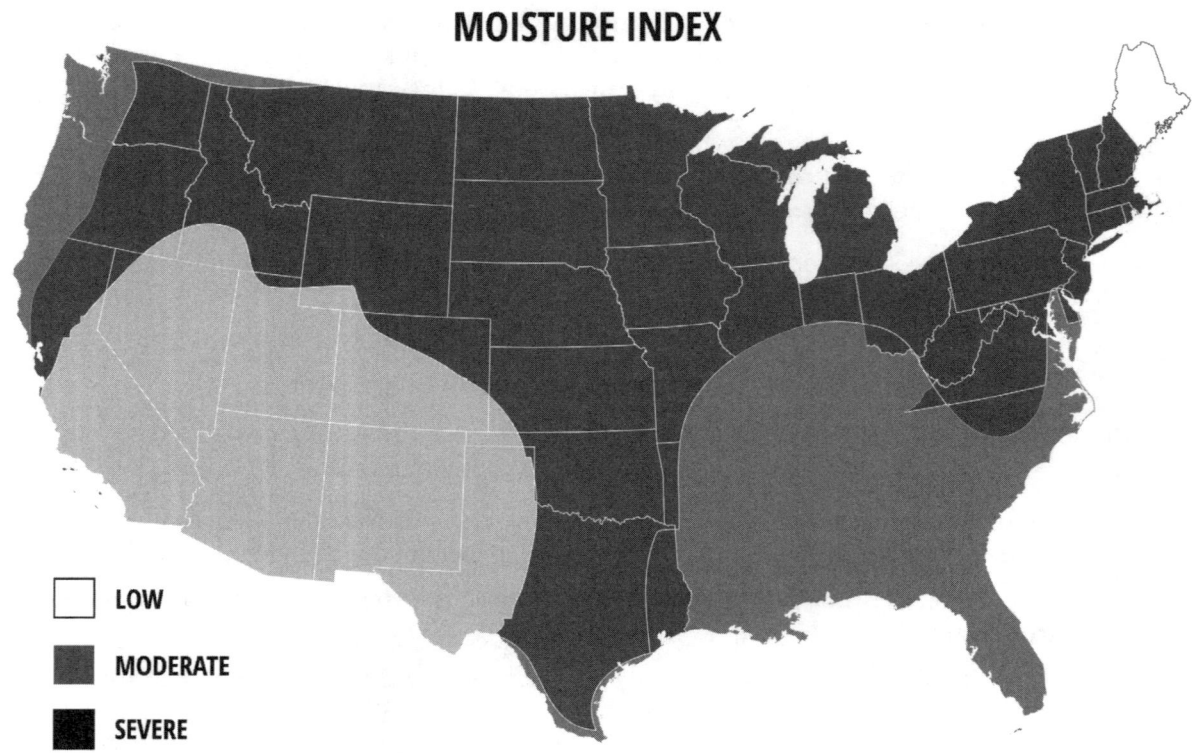

☐ LOW

■ MODERATE

■ SEVERE

STEP 2: Assess Building Exposure

The terrain surrounding a building impacts its exposure to wind-driven rain. The ratio of roof overhang width to the height of the protected wall below also alters the exposure of a building to weather and wind-driven rain. Long roof overhangs relative to wall height effectively reduce the exposure. Similarly, increased shielding of the site against wind tends to reduce the effects of climate.

Table 7 may be used to determine a building's exposure level based on the climate condition determined in Step 1, the roof overhang ratio, and the wind exposure. The exposure level then leads to a reasonable weather-resistant envelope approach in Step 3. The exposure levels in Table 7 can also be used on a smaller scale to get a sense of the exposure for particular faces of a building, or even for specific envelope elements, such as a window.

Understanding the exposure in this manner can guide inspections of flashing details, the potential benefits of having greater overhangs installed, etc.

Table 7 - Building Exposure Levels (H = high; M = moderate; L = low; N = negligible exposure)				
Wind Exposure	**Overhang Ratio[a] (w/h)**	**Climate Severity[b] (from Step 1)**		
		Severe	**Moderate**	**Low**
No Shielding (Open)	0	H	H	M
	0.1	H	M	L
	0.2	M	L	L
	0.3	M	L	N
	0.4	L	L	N
	≥0.5	L	N	N
Partial Shielding (Typical Suburban)	0	H	H	M
	0.1	H	M	L
	0.2	M	L	N
	0.3	L	N	N
	0.4	L	N	N
	≥0.5	N	N	N
Full Shielding	0	H	H	M
	0.1	M	M	L
	0.2	L	L	N
	0.3	L	N	N
	0.4	N	N	N
	≥0.5	N	N	N

a. Overhang ratio should account for both roof overhangs and overhangs from cantilevered floors. For a given wall, use the worst-case overhang ratio (w/h) where "w" is the overhang width and "h" is the height of the wall below the overhang.

b. For buildings located near the top of topographic features, such as ridges, bluffs, and escarpments, the building exposure level should be increased by one level.

The wind exposure conditions in Table 7 are explained as follows:

- A no-shielding (or open) site receives little or no protection from surrounding buildings and natural obstructions to wind flow (such as grassy fields or waterfront exposure).

- A partial-shielding site receives protection from typical suburban development, including surroundings of homes, and natural and man-made landscaping, such as interspersed trees of similar or greater height than the buildings.

- A full-shielding site receives significant protection from surrounding dense development (more than four homes per acre) and/or closely spaced trees (e.g., generally more than 15 to 20 large trees per acre) extending for a horizontal distance of at least 10 building-heights from the building.

STEP 3: Weather-Resistant Envelope

Based on the building exposure level determined in Step 2, a WRE approach may be selected and installed based on expectations of relative performance. Alternatively, other factors may be reconsidered in the building and site design to improve protection from rain, such as the use of larger overhangs to protect walls.

Table 8 - Relative Performance of WRE Approaches				
Exposure Level (from Table 7)	Face-Sealed	Concealed Barrier	Drained Cavity	Basic Rainscreen
High (H)	Poor	Poor	Fair	Good
Moderate (M)	Poor	Fair	Good	Good
Low (L)	Fair	Good	Good	Good
Negligible	Good	Good	Good	Good
a. Refer to the course on "mass wall" systems used as a weather-resistant barrier.				

The ratings used in Table 8 may be subject to adjustment by experience. Relative performance is explained as follows:

- good: The WRE system is likely to meet or exceed acceptable performance expectations and has a low risk of failure during the likely service life, with a reasonable level of installation quality and maintenance.
- fair: The WRE system is considered adequate but may require careful attention to detailing, installation quality and maintenance. The wall has a tolerable risk of failure during the likely service life.
- poor: The WRE system has a relatively high risk of not meeting acceptable performance expectations.

These ratings don't take into account numerous other factors, including the variation in construction of various systems, the durability of cladding and other wall components, or the reliability of expected maintenance. Therefore, the ratings may be subject to adjustment by experience.

Solid or mass walls, such as masonry and concrete wall systems without a separate exterior cladding, are not addressed in Table 8. These walls rely on deflection of rain as well as the ability to absorb moisture in a sufficiently thick and durable wall system. However, even these "mass" walls can become overwhelmed with moisture intake during extreme wind-driven rain episodes (e.g., hurricanes and tropical storms). Water-repellent surface treatments or coatings like latex paint may be applied to these walls to improve rain deflection and minimize absorption of moisture; however, such coatings should be semi-permeable to allow for drying toward the outside. Various water-repellent treatments are available for concrete and masonry, but they vary in cost, performance, and effective service life. Limited research indicates that polysiloxane-blended water repellents may provide the best water repellency and durability.

Checking Windows and Doors

Checking Window and Door Components

The three major window and door frame types used in conventional residential construction are wood, vinyl and aluminum. Windows and doors can be key contributors to water penetration in walls from either flashing failures around these components or characteristics of the components themselves. This section discusses the features of window and door components that may reduce leakage and related moisture problems. Without careful installation of window and door components, it should be assumed that they will leak some amount of water into the wall cavity.

Simply relying on window and door products that are labeled according to standard test methods does not necessarily guarantee that water leakage will not occur through their frames into walls. Frames that rely on seals and sealants at internal and exposed joints will eventually leak water as these joints fail over time. The life expectancy of window and door units may vary widely, from 10 to 50+ years, depending on unit type and materials, exposure, maintenance, types of seals and sealants used at joints, and other factors. Frames that rely on "welding" of joints rather than sealants will generally provide a longer moisture-resistant service life.

Checking the Manufacturer's Installation Guidelines

Many performance problems with windows and doors are related to installation issues. Installation directions included with window and door units should be followed carefully. Home inspectors are not required to confirm compliance with a manufacturer's recommendations. However, knowing the general guidelines and techniques for proper installation of windows and doors will assist the inspector in recognizing installation problems that may promote moisture intrusion.

Many units have weeps that allow water to discharge from the unit. These weeps should be free from construction debris and appropriately arranged relative to siding and flashing to drain water away from the wall.

In the absence of relevant installation details for a specific application and combination of exterior envelope materials, the manufacturer should be consulted. In addition, industry-standard installation guidelines may be consulted, such as ASTM E2112-01.

Tip Regarding Caulking of Nail Flanges

Caulking of nail flanges (particularly at the window head and jambs) is critical to the prevention of moisture intrusion and commonly used nail flange windows. This is particularly important if the flashing recommendations previously discussed are not used. Thus, proper window flange caulking practices should be the subject of inspection and training during the installation process.

Field-Test Repetitive Installations on Large Projects

Field testing is far beyond the scope of a typical home inspection. However, understanding field testing can be valuable for an inspector who may be diagnosing moisture intrusion problems. Field testing of window and door products and their actual installation is one of the best ways to assess water-resistance. The tests may involve a simple water spray test using a garden hose, or using a standard field-test method, such as the ASTM E1105-00, known as "Field Determination of Water Penetration of Installed Exterior Curtain Walls and Doors by Uniform or Cyclic Static Air Pressure Difference." If a simple hose spray test is used, keep in mind that the test should mimic realistic rainfall conditions or the results won't be very meaningful. The more stringent ASTM field test is perhaps only justified on production home installation details that will be used repetitively. Mock-ups of details may also be used for this purpose (see ASTM E2099-00). General guidance for evaluating water leakage problems, as well as commissioning of building envelopes, is also available (see ASTM E2128-01a and ASTM E241-00).

Inspectors Should Know How Windows and Doors Manage Water

There are marked differences in how window and door units manage water. Under wind-driven rain conditions, water will penetrate window frame crevices and seals between the sash and the frame. Under severe conditions, this water may even be forced through the window joints into the interior side of the window. Windows that perform best have adequate clearances between the sashes and frame to allow water to freely drain, rather than becoming trapped. A minimum gap of about 1/4-inch is recommended to prevent capillary action from holding moisture in locations where it can be driven by wind-pressure differentials past seals and through frame joints. In addition, high-performance windows have a system for weeping intruded water that acts much like a rainscreen wall system. In severe wind-driven rain conditions (such as high-exposure conditions), high-performance window and door systems are preferred for the same reasons that cavity and rainscreen WRE systems are preferred. The recommendations above detailing window and door frames can generally be checked by inspecting the manufacturer's technical specifications showing a cross-section of the unit, including dimensions, seals, thermal breaks (if included), and other factors that may create leakage paths, such as corner frame joints and mulled joints in a multiple window assembly.

What Are Third Party-Certified Products?

The level of performance and certification of window and door components varies a great deal. You typically get what you pay for. Current building codes generally require that window and glass door products comply with the 101/I.S.2/NAFS-02 Standard, as verified and labeled by an independent certification agency and laboratory. Furthermore, products that do not fall within the scope of that standard are required to be at least tested in accordance with ASTM E330 for water- and wind-pressure resistance. Unfortunately, these standards do not necessarily require periodic sampling of production units, and manufacturers' quality control may vary. The use of third party-certified products, however, should reduce the likelihood of receiving substandard components. Various entities provide window and door certification and labeling services, such as the American Architectural Manufacturers Association (AAMA), and the Window and Door Manufacturers Association (WDMA).

Wind-Pressure and Impact-Resistance Ratings

Glazing in windows and doors should meet the requirements for wind-pressure loading. Wind pressure requirements are found in the local building code for the wind region (for design wind speed) corresponding to the house's location. Product labeling and certification should indicate the appropriate wind-pressure rating. In areas that are identified as "wind-borne debris regions" (including hurricane-prone coastal areas), the local building code may also require the use of wind-borne debris protection (such as shutters), or impact-resistant glazing. Such units are required to comply with ASTM E1886 and ASTM E1996 standards, which also should be indicated on product labeling and certifications. In many cases, field-supplied structural wood panel coverings with a suitable attachment method are acceptable. Impact-rated shutter systems, both manual and automatic, are also available.

Flashing of Wall Components

The Flashing of Wall Components and Moisture Problems

Water penetration and accumulation in walls are most commonly associated with flashing and detailing problems around windows, doors and other penetrations through the weather-resistant wall envelope. This section provides recommended flashing details for common applications in residential construction. These points are intended to enhance the inspector's knowledge and to help fulfill the basic objective for flashing of the weather-resistant wall envelope, as found in the 2006 IRC:

> R703.8 Flashing. Approved corrosion-resistive flashing shall be provided in the exterior wall envelope in such a manner as to prevent entry of water into the wall cavity, or penetration of water to the building structural framing components. The flashing shall extend to the surface of the exterior wall finish. Approved corrosion-resistant flashings shall be installed at all of the following locations:
>
> 1. exterior window and door openings: Flashing at exterior window and door openings shall extend to the surface of the exterior wall finish or to the water-resistive barrier for subsequent drainage;
>
> 2. at the intersection of chimneys or other masonry construction with frame or stucco walls, with projecting lips on both sides under stucco copings;
>
> 3. under and at the ends of masonry, wood or metal copings and sills;
>
> 4. continuously above all projecting wood trim;
>
> 5. where exterior porches, decks or stairs attach to a wall or floor assembly of wood-frame construction;
>
> 6. at wall and roof intersections; and
>
> 7. at built-in gutters.

Understanding and Inspecting Flashing Details for Windows, Doors and Ledgers

In the images on the following two pages, some typical yet very important flashing details are provided as general models for correct installation techniques. These are not presented as the only solutions to flashing — because there are certainly many other viable solutions — but as examples of workable approaches to protecting shell penetrations from water intrusion.

Flashing details for windows and deck ledgers are essential for preventing water damage to wall assemblies. The kick-out flashing detail depicted earlier is important to protect against water intrusion. A variety of manufactured window sill and door threshold flashing components (such as pre-molded pan flashings) are also available in lieu of site-built flashing components featured in this section. These components are used to expel any water leakage at the base of windows and doors. Recommendations that address different building conditions can be found in the Energy and Environmental Building Association's (EEBA) Water Management Guide, and various other industry resources.

Illustrations

The following two images illustrate window flashing details that can be used depending on when the windows are installed relative to the envelope's weather barrier (housewrap or building paper).

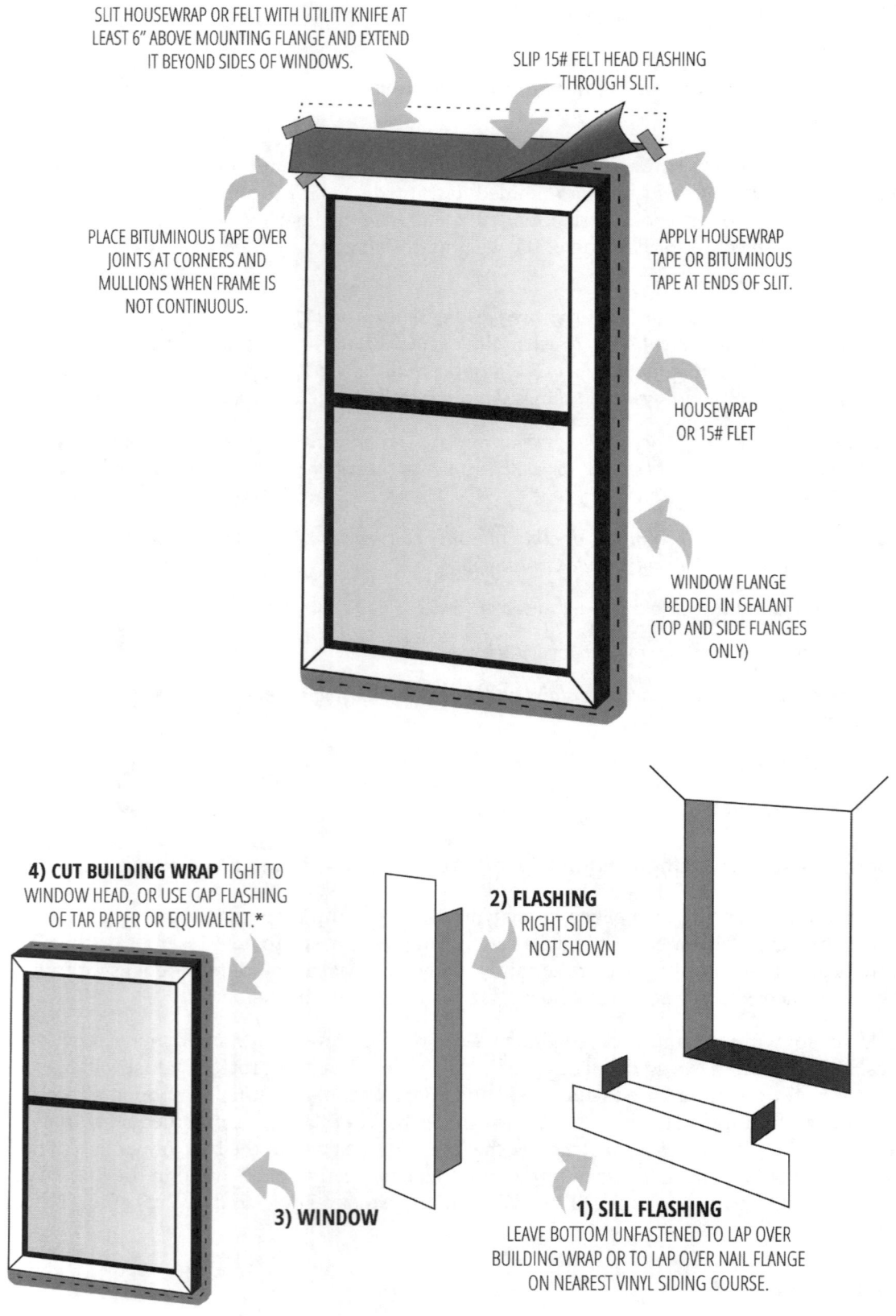

SLIT HOUSEWRAP OR FELT WITH UTILITY KNIFE AT LEAST 6" ABOVE MOUNTING FLANGE AND EXTEND IT BEYOND SIDES OF WINDOWS.

SLIP 15# FELT HEAD FLASHING THROUGH SLIT.

PLACE BITUMINOUS TAPE OVER JOINTS AT CORNERS AND MULLIONS WHEN FRAME IS NOT CONTINUOUS.

APPLY HOUSEWRAP TAPE OR BITUMINOUS TAPE AT ENDS OF SLIT.

HOUSEWRAP OR 15# FLET

WINDOW FLANGE BEDDED IN SEALANT (TOP AND SIDE FLANGES ONLY)

4) CUT BUILDING WRAP TIGHT TO WINDOW HEAD, OR USE CAP FLASHING OF TAR PAPER OR EQUIVALENT.*

2) FLASHING RIGHT SIDE NOT SHOWN

3) WINDOW

1) SILL FLASHING LEAVE BOTTOM UNFASTENED TO LAP OVER BUILDING WRAP OR TO LAP OVER NAIL FLANGE ON NEAREST VINYL SIDING COURSE.

* CAP OR HEAD FLASHING, IF NOT IN A BUILDING WITH A CONTINUOUS SECONDARY WEATHER BARRIER, MUST TERMINATE AT THE TOP OF THE WALL OR BELOW AN AREA PROTECTED BY A ROOF OVERHANG.

In the first image below, the enhanced flashing details at the jamb and the sill are designed to provide enhanced protection against water intrusion in more severe weather conditions.

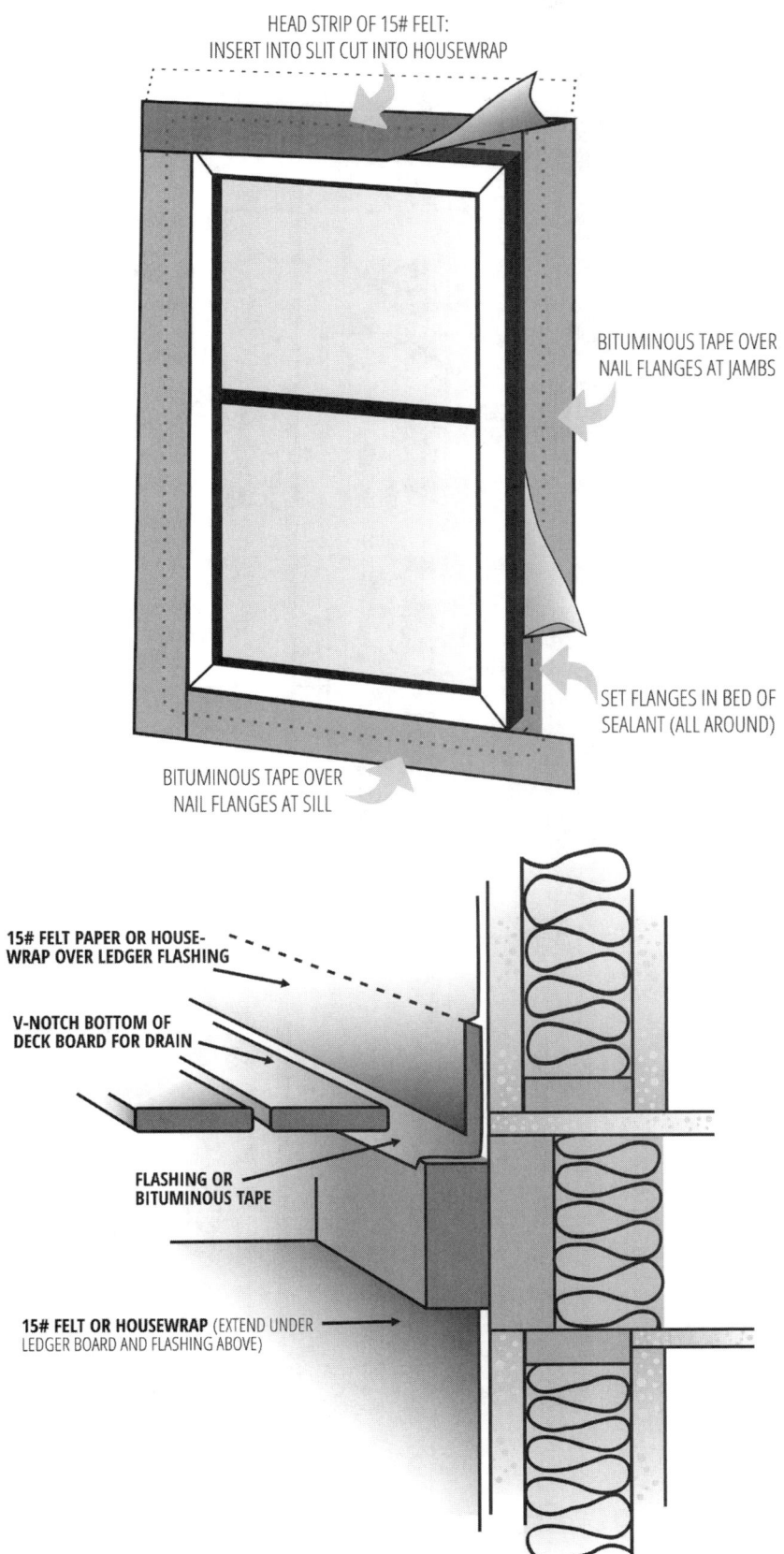

HEAD STRIP OF 15# FELT:
INSERT INTO SLIT CUT INTO HOUSEWRAP

BITUMINOUS TAPE OVER
NAIL FLANGES AT JAMBS

SET FLANGES IN BED OF
SEALANT (ALL AROUND)

BITUMINOUS TAPE OVER
NAIL FLANGES AT SILL

15# FELT PAPER OR HOUSE-
WRAP OVER LEDGER FLASHING

V-NOTCH BOTTOM OF
DECK BOARD FOR DRAIN

FLASHING OR
BITUMINOUS TAPE

15# FELT OR HOUSEWRAP (EXTEND UNDER
LEDGER BOARD AND FLASHING ABOVE)

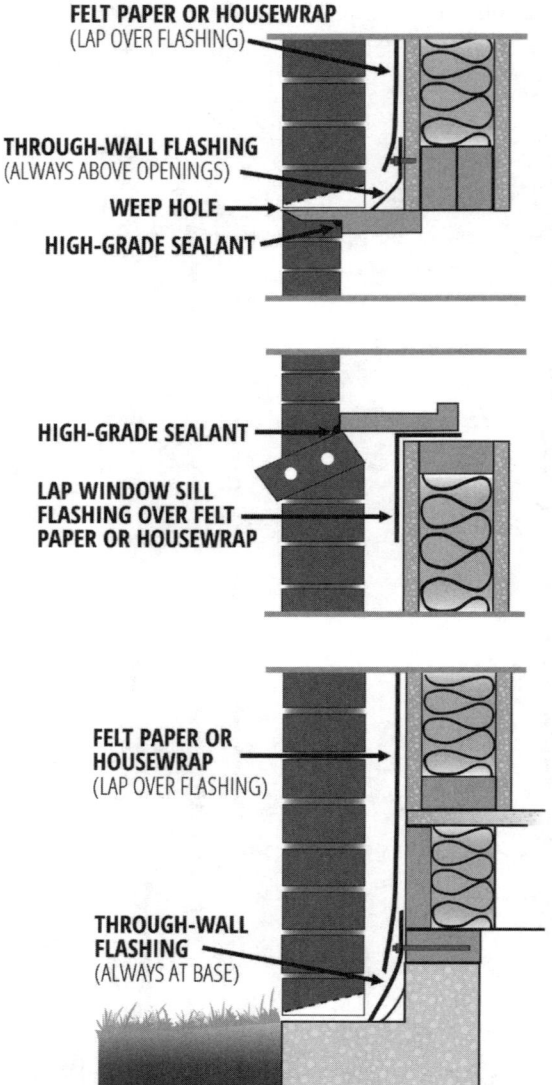

FELT PAPER OR HOUSEWRAP
(LAP OVER FLASHING)

THROUGH-WALL FLASHING
(ALWAYS ABOVE OPENINGS)

WEEP HOLE

HIGH-GRADE SEALANT

HIGH-GRADE SEALANT

LAP WINDOW SILL FLASHING OVER FELT PAPER OR HOUSEWRAP

FELT PAPER OR HOUSEWRAP
(LAP OVER FLASHING)

THROUGH-WALL FLASHING
(ALWAYS AT BASE)

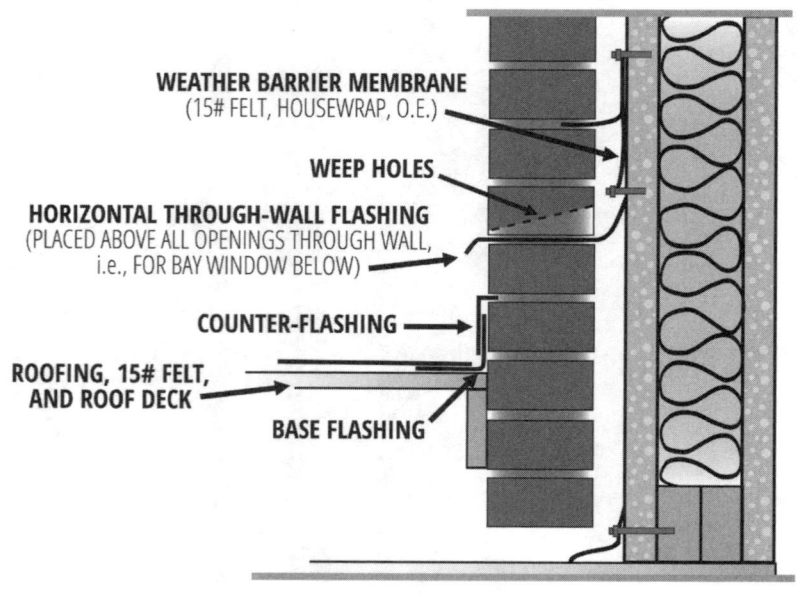

WEATHER BARRIER MEMBRANE
(15# FELT, HOUSEWRAP, O.E.)

WEEP HOLES

HORIZONTAL THROUGH-WALL FLASHING
(PLACED ABOVE ALL OPENINGS THROUGH WALL,
i.e., FOR BAY WINDOW BELOW)

COUNTER-FLASHING

ROOFING, 15# FELT, AND ROOF DECK

BASE FLASHING

Checking Caulks and Sealants

Inspection of Caulks and Sealants

In the construction of the weather-resistant envelope (WRE) system, there will be joints and seams that require or at least benefit from the appropriate use and maintenance of caulks and sealants. In the absence of guidelines for specification and application of caulk and sealants in model building codes, this section provides valuable information for inspectors regarding their use. Where caulk is required by a manufacturer's installation instructions, the specified caulk materials and methods should be followed carefully by the installer and then checked by the inspector.

In general, caulks and sealants should not be relied on as the primary defense against water intrusion at joints in a WRE system. Flashing is preferred wherever feasible, even when caulk is additionally used. Standard-quality caulk and application practices, combined with the shrinkage and swelling of the building's components, usually result in the onset of gradual failure of the watertight seal within a few years.

Air Sealing

Caulking can prevent water damage inside and outside of the home when applied around faucets, ceiling fixtures, water pipes, drains, bathtubs, and other plumbing fixtures. Caulking can also be used to seal air leakage. Before applying caulking in an existing home, the homeowner should detect major air leakage and assess ventilation needs to ensure adequate indoor air quality.

Selecting Caulk

Most caulking compounds come in disposable cartridges that fit in half-barrel caulking guns (if possible, purchase one with an automatic release). Some pressurized cartridges do not require caulking guns.

When deciding how much caulking to use, the homeowner should consider that they'll probably need a half-cartridge per window or door and four cartridges for the foundation sill of an average home. Caulking compounds can also be found in aerosol cans, squeeze tubes, and ropes for small jobs or special applications.

Caulking compounds vary in strength, properties, and price. Water-based caulk can be cleaned with water, while solvent-based compounds require a solvent for cleanup. See the table to follow for information about common caulking compounds.

Common Caulking Compounds

Caulking Compound	Recommended Uses	Cleanup	Shrinkage	Adhesion	Cost	Comments
Silicone: Household	Seals joints between bath and kitchen fixtures and tile. Forms adhesive for tiles and metal fixtures. Seals metal joints, such as those in plumbing and gutters.	Dry cloth if immediate; mineral spirits or naphtha	Little or none	Good to excellent	High	Flexible: cured silicone allows stretch joints up to three times normal width or compression to one-half the width.
Silicone: Construction	Seals most dissimilar building materials, such as wood and stone, metal flashing, and brick.	Dry cloth if immediate; mineral spirits or naphtha	Little or none	Good to excellent	High	Permits joints to stretch or compress. Silicones will stick to painted surfaces, but paint will not adhere to most cured silicones.
Polyurethane, expandable spray foam	Expands when curing; good for larger cracks indoors or outdoors. Use in non-friction areas, as material can become dry and powdery over time.	Solvent such as lacquer thinner, if immediate	None; expands quite a bit	Good to excellent	Moderate to high	Spray foam quickly expands to fit larger, irregular gaps. Flexible. Can be applied at variable temperatures. Must be painted for exterior use to protect from ultraviolet radiation. Manufacturing process produces greenhouse gases.
Water-based foam sealant	Around window and door frames in new construction; smaller cracks	Water	None; expands only 25%	Good to excellent	High	Takes 24 hours to cure. Cures to soft consistency. Water-based foam production does not produce greenhouse gases. Will not over-expand to bend windows (new construction). Must be exposed to air to dry. Not useful for larger gaps, as curing becomes difficult.

Caulking Compound	Recommended Uses	Cleanup	Shrinkage	Adhesion	Cost	Comments
Butyl rubber	Seals most dissimilar materials (glass, metal, plastic, wood, and concrete). Seals around windows and flashing, bonds loose shingles.	Mineral spirits or naphtha	From 5% to 30%	Good	Moderate to high	Durable 10 or more years; resilient, not brittle. Can be painted after one week curing. Variable shrinkage; may require two applications. Does not adhere well to painted surfaces. Toxic; follow label precautions.
Latex	Seals joints around tub and shower. Fills cracks in tile, plaster, glass, and plastic; fills nail holes.	Water	From 5% to 10%	Good to excellent	Moderate	Easy to use. Seams can be trimmed or smoothed with moist finger or tool. Water-resistant when dry. Can be sanded and painted. Less elastic than above materials. Varied durability, 2–10 years. Will not adhere to metal. Little flexibility once cured. Needs to be painted when used on exteriors.
Oil- or resin-based	Seals exterior seams and joints on building materials.	Mineral spirits or naphtha	From 10% to 20%	Good	Low	Readily available. Least expensive of the four types. Rope and tube form available. Oils dry out and cause material to harden and fall out. Low durability, 1–4 years. Poor adhesion to porous surfaces like masonry. Should be painted. Can be toxic (check label). Limited temperature range.

Applying Caulk

Although not a high-tech operation, caulking can be tricky. Read and follow the instructions on the compound cartridge, and remember these tips:

- For good adhesion, clean all areas to be caulked. Remove any old caulk and paint using a putty knife, large screwdriver, stiff brush, or special solvent. Make sure the area is dry so you don't seal in moisture.

- Apply caulk to all joints in a window frame and the joint between the frame and the wall.
- Hold the gun at a consistent angle. Forty-five degrees is best for getting deep into the crack. You know you've got the right angle when the caulk is immediately forced into the crack as it comes out of the tube.
- Caulk in one straight continuous stream, if possible. Avoid stops and starts.
- Send caulk to the bottom of an opening to avoid bubbles.
- Make sure the caulk sticks to both sides of a crack or seam.
- Release the trigger before pulling the gun away to avoid applying too much caulking compound. A caulking gun with an automatic release makes this much easier.
- If caulk oozes out of a crack, use a putty knife to push it back in.
- Don't skimp. If the caulk shrinks, reapply it to form a smooth bead that will seal the crack completely.

The best time to apply caulk is during dry weather when the outdoor temperature is above 45° F (7.2° C). Low humidity is important during application to prevent cracks from swelling with moisture. Warm temperatures are also necessary so the caulk will set properly and adhere to the surfaces.

Face-Sealed WRE

For face-sealed WRE systems, the appropriate sealant specification and installation are critical. Manufacturers' recommendations for cladding and sealant should have been followed when the window was installed. The recommendations should specify window and door components (drainage features and frame materials) that are compatible with face-sealed WRE applications, as well as the specified caulk. For example, welded-seam aluminum window frames with exterior drainage and internal pressure-equalization features are commonly used in commercial building applications with face-sealed WRE systems.

Checking for Appropriate Sealants

Some general information regarding the type of caulks and sealants is provided in Table 9, including longevity, the best uses, and the appropriate types of joints for given sealants. With proper adherence to the manufacturers' instructions, particularly with respect to surface preparation, high-quality caulks and sealants can be made to endure for a reasonable length of time between maintenance and replacement — up to five years, or considerably longer when not severely exposed. Silicone rubber and urethane caulks generally give the best overall performance for applications to exterior building envelopes. For bath and shower applications, mildew-resistant silicone caulks are also available.

Caulks and sealants should be stored in a warm environment and should not be stored for more than a couple of years before use. A high-quality caulk installation requires appropriate ambient temperature, dry and clean surfaces, and an adequate joint gap to allow the caulk to act elastically without pulling loose from the two caulked parts. In addition, foam backer rod or bond-breaker tape may be installed to create an appropriate caulk joint profile for adhesion, flexibility and durability. Inspection of caulking is strongly recommended.

Moisture-Resistant Foundations

Checking the Site and Foundation

A building site (the grounds surrounding the structure) is a vital factor in providing for a moisture-resistant home. Assessing the moisture and drainage conditions at a home is perhaps the first and most important step in inspecting for a moisture-resistant foundation. Building foundations should be located on sites in a manner that prevents moisture problems by providing for adequate drainage of on- and off-site surface water flows, including roof water runoff. Groundwater conditions should also be considered during an inspection of a home with moisture-related problems. The foundation type, foundation elevations, and foundation moisture-resistant detailing are related factors that are dependent on a number of site characteristics.

Many sites are considered "normal" and fall within standard conditions addressed in the residential building code. However, the use of marginal sites — which is becoming more common — without the proper site design can result in costly mistakes, such as foundation, structural and moisture problems. Appropriate foundation elevations and drainage patterns for the site should be considered.

Check the Site's Drainage

When a house is built, a site plan should be developed to do more than just locate the building and utilities, and demonstrate compliance with setbacks and other zoning requirements. The site plan should also account for a drainage plan that indicates the slope of land and drainage patterns that convey surface waters from the building site. For sites that generally provide natural drainage away from the building's location, the main concern is establishing an appropriate foundation elevation to maintain drainage immediately adjacent to the foundation.

Model building standards typically require a minimum of 6 inches of fall in ground level over a distance of 10 feet from the perimeter of the building. Providing for additional slope is a good method to offset future settlement of foundation backfill next to the building, unless the soil is moderately compacted or tamped during the backfill process.

Conditions that warrant careful consideration by an inspector on any site include:

- high local water table (within 4 to 8 feet of the lowest proposed foundation floor/grade level);
- natural depressions that collect or channel on- and off-site flows;
- springs or wet areas on site;
- soft or loose soils, indicative of poor bearing capacity;
- development that will result in more than 10% to 20% of impervious area coverage on the site;
- steep slopes (greater than 25%) that may be unstable or easily eroded;
- signs of existing erosion (gullies, slope failures, etc.);
- sensitive areas that may be impacted by proposed development, such as natural streams, wetlands or other features;
- off-site surface water flows directed onto and across the proposed site;
- inadequate building offset from adjacent steep slopes that generate increased surface water runoff. A minimum offset of 15 feet from the toe of a 1:3 or 33% or greater slope is generally recommended, but special conditions may warrant a greater or lesser amount of offset; and
- 100-year floodplain located on site or near the building's location.

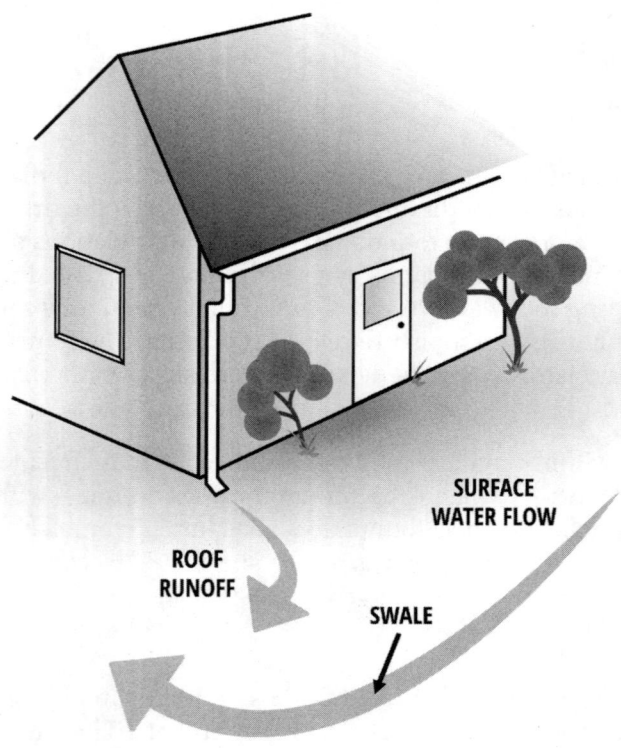

SURFACE WATER FLOW

ROOF RUNOFF

SWALE

Poor site drainage of surface water is perhaps the most important contributor to foundation moisture problems. Thus, the factors listed above should be considered during an inspection.

Wetness of the site, soil-bearing conditions, and slope of the site are key factors in making a decision on whether to build and how to build the house. When poor site conditions exist, they can often be overcome technically, provided there are no land-use restrictions.

However, the added cost of design and non-conventional foundation construction (such as an elevated foundation and/or special drainage features) should be considered important aspects of the expense of building a house. It is usually very costly to correct site drainage problems and foundation moisture issues after the fact. Therefore, the inspector must be very careful as to what recommendations s/he makes about a site with poor drainage.

Further Evaluation of the Site by a Professional

Fortunately, a site's potential for moisture problems can be screened relatively quickly by:

- interviewing adjacent and/or previous property owners;
- conducting a site exploration, including shallow soil borings (to assess soil-bearing strength), and water table assessment to several feet below the proposed foundation depths;
- understanding the history of local foundation practices used in the vicinity of the proposed site;
- reviewing publicly available soil survey reports published by the USDA's Natural Resources Conservation Service (formerly known as the Soil Conservation Service). These reports from the Soil Data Mart are published for most counties and address soil characteristics and provide general land-use recommendations;
- reviewing local topography for drainage patterns (such as USGS topographical maps, available for free on **www.topozone.com**); and
- observing the site during or immediately following a significant rainfall event that produces excess rainfall.

Ask the Builder

In one builder survey, about 75% of builders that reported basement leakage problems had not conducted water table tests prior to construction.

If any initial screening observations indicate the potential existence of site conditions mentioned previously, the site should be more carefully investigated by a geotechnical engineer or other qualified professional familiar with local building practices and ground conditions. The foundation plan should be based on the results of the findings. For a site considered to be normal (absent of such conditions), minimum foundation moisture-resistant practices in modern building codes are usually adequate. The best practices featured later in this section provide enhanced performance in comparison to minimum-accepted practices for foundation design.

Inspecting the Basement Foundation

Moisture problems are frequently found in the basement of a home or building. Even in some of the driest of site conditions, foundations are continually exposed to moisture vapor from the ground. When basements are used inappropriately on sites with high groundwater, or in areas with intermittent periods of higher ground moisture levels due to rainfall and water table fluctuations, they are frequently exposed to bulk water. Therefore, foundations must be detailed to deal with the potential for water leakage through cracks and joints, capillary movement of water through foundation materials, vapor transmission of moisture through foundation materials, and condensation of moist air on cool foundation surfaces. The degree of protection required for any given site and selected foundation type is primarily a judgment call by the inspector in determining whether it meets or exceeds minimum building code requirements. The building standards and recommendations in this section are intended to teach enhanced moisture-resistance techniques. Interior finishing and insulation of basement walls are addressed later in this section.

Foundations that create below-ground spaces on wet sites are of particular concern. During an inspection, an inspector may find evidence of attempts to remedy moisture problems by painstaking waterproofing efforts that may ultimately have a shorter life than the building. As a rule of thumb, moisture protection of foundations by the owner or builder should err on the conservative side when there is reasonable doubt as to the moisture conditions on site. The moisture-resistant practices presented in this manual are for the inspector to use as a resource. They can be used for consideration during the construction of a building. They are quite inexpensive compared to the cost of correcting moisture problems after construction is completed. They also reduce the risk of moisture problems in other parts of the building by protecting a prominent entry point for moisture: the foundation.

Illustrations

The illustrations on the next page and the following sections highlight details for moisture-resistant basement foundations that inspectors can look for during an inspection. These details can be used in diagnosing moisture-related problems that may be discovered. Most of these details will not be readily visible to a home inspector during an inspection of an existing structure, but may be observable during the construction phase when the building materials and components are exposed and open for inspection.

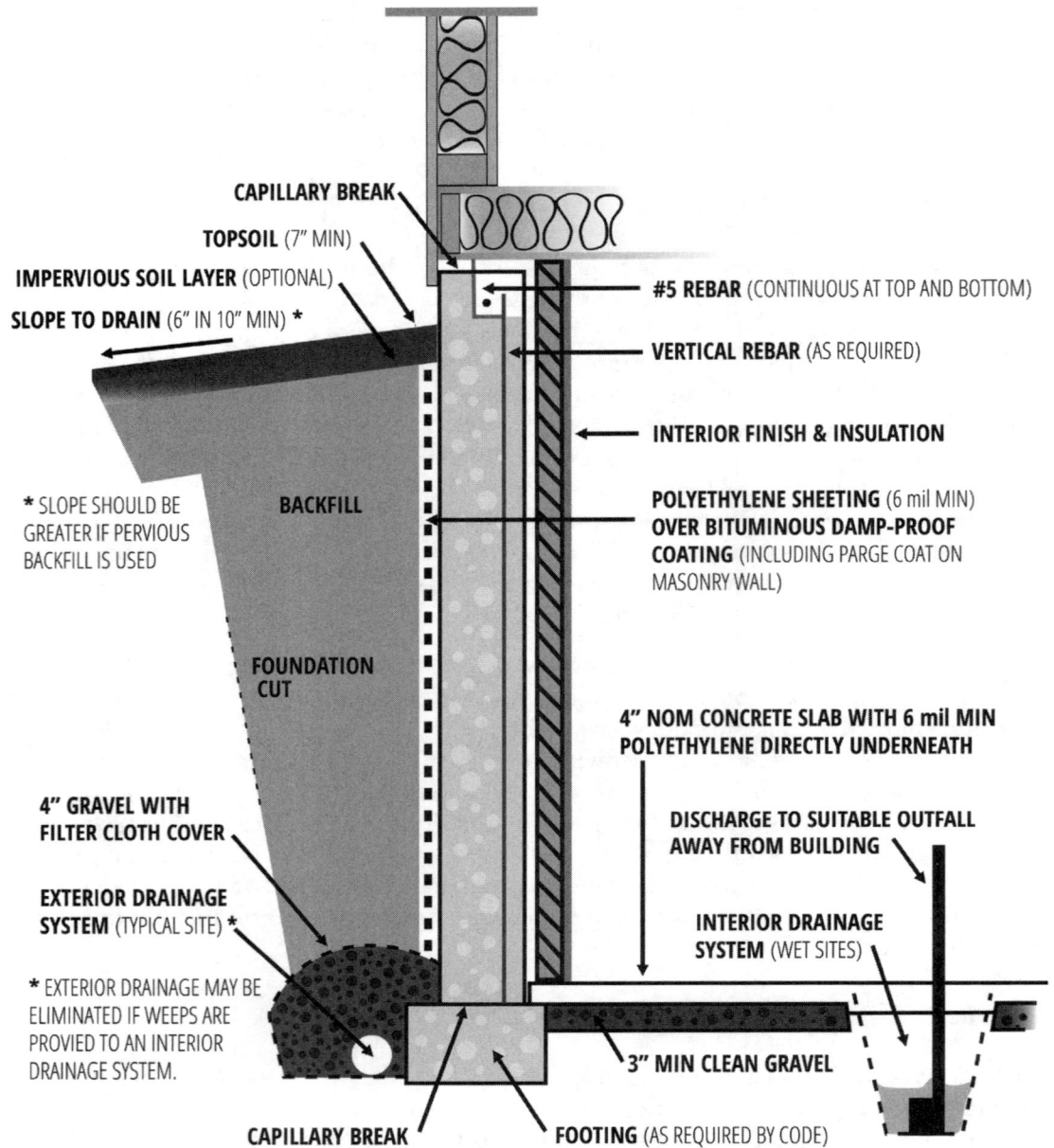

CAPILLARY BREAK

TOPSOIL (7" MIN)

IMPERVIOUS SOIL LAYER (OPTIONAL)

SLOPE TO DRAIN (6" IN 10" MIN) *

#5 REBAR (CONTINUOUS AT TOP AND BOTTOM)

VERTICAL REBAR (AS REQUIRED)

INTERIOR FINISH & INSULATION

* SLOPE SHOULD BE GREATER IF PERVIOUS BACKFILL IS USED

BACKFILL

POLYETHYLENE SHEETING (6 mil MIN) OVER BITUMINOUS DAMP-PROOF COATING (INCLUDING PARGE COAT ON MASONRY WALL)

FOUNDATION CUT

4" NOM CONCRETE SLAB WITH 6 mil MIN POLYETHYLENE DIRECTLY UNDERNEATH

4" GRAVEL WITH FILTER CLOTH COVER

DISCHARGE TO SUITABLE OUTFALL AWAY FROM BUILDING

EXTERIOR DRAINAGE SYSTEM (TYPICAL SITE) *

INTERIOR DRAINAGE SYSTEM (WET SITES)

* EXTERIOR DRAINAGE MAY BE ELIMINATED IF WEEPS ARE PROVIED TO AN INTERIOR DRAINAGE SYSTEM.

3" MIN CLEAN GRAVEL

CAPILLARY BREAK

FOOTING (AS REQUIRED BY CODE)

Inspection of Drainage Slopes and Understanding Backfill

Proper grading to provide positive flow of surface water and roof water runoff (or gutter discharge) is one of the simplest and most important features to provide on a building site. When possible, the minimum 6-inch fall in finish grade over a distance of 10 feet from the building (minimum 5% slope) should be exceeded and extended. This is particularly important if backfill practices are not reasonably controlled to prevent settlement. On very flat sites, this may require mounding of the foundation pad, and coordination of appropriate foundation elevations to promote drainage. On sloped sites, excavation and grading in the up-slope direction must provide for sufficient drainage away from the building perimeter and against the direction of natural water flow on the site. For sites with very steep slopes, this may require the use of a retaining wall at the toe of a steep slope.

Backfill & Site Grading Problems Make for Wet Basements

In one survey of basement leakage problems, about 85% of the moisture problems appeared only after rain storms or melting snow—a strong indication of the importance of site drainage in preventing foundation moisture problems. Of these incidences of basement leakage problems, about 40% were associated with improper surface grading, 25% were related to improper downspout drainage, and another 25% were associated with settling of backfill resulting in improper surface grading after passage of time (often within the first year after construction). Thus, a majority of basement water problems are associated with backfill and site grading.

Backfill soil should be placed in a manner that prevents settlement and potential surface-water flow toward the foundation. This may require that backfill soil be placed in 6- to 8-inch layers or lifts, and then compacted with light-construction equipment, or tamped to prevent settlement over time. A heavy compaction effort (typical for commercial building or roadway construction) should not be promoted, as this may damage typical residential foundation walls. The goal is to compact sufficiently to prevent future settlement from the process of natural consolidation of loosely placed soil. In addition, backfill should not be placed without first installing the floor system (or temporary bracing) to support the foundation walls.

Finally, the upper layers of the backfill should be of moderate, low-permeability soil (e.g., with some clay content) to help reduce the direct infiltration of rainwater adjacent to the foundation. Where only pervious soils are available for backfill, the slope of grade away from the perimeter of the foundation should be increased, or an impervious "skirt" of 6-mil polyethylene may be placed about 12 inches below grade.

Good Backfill

It is notoriously difficult to control grading and backfilling operations in typical residential construction. On many sites, the common practice is to place the backfill with the least amount of effort required to merely fill the hole. Proper backfill practices and grading will ensure that the foundation remains dry to a greater degree than all the other recommendations here.

Understanding Foundation Drainage Systems

Foundation drainage serves a number of roles. First, it removes free water from the foundation's perimeter, which reduces the lateral (sideways) load on the foundation wall. It also lowers the groundwater level in the vicinity of the building's footprint, should it become elevated above the basement floor level during a particularly wet season or year. Remember that basements should not be used where groundwater levels are near the basement's floor level.

Current model building codes require that drains be provided around all foundations that enclose habitable space (such as basements). However, exceptions are made for soils that are naturally well-draining. Unless a site-specific soil investigation is done, or extensive local experience confirms that groundwater levels are consistently deep, soils should not be assumed to be well-draining.

Where the foundation drainage system cannot be drained to daylight by gravity, a sump and pump must be used to collect the water and discharge it to a suitable outfall (such as a rock pad and swale) a safe distance away from the building foundation. Furthermore, use of a drainage layer underneath the entire basement floor slab, coupled with weeps to a drainage system around the outside perimeter of the foundation, may be a more effective way to eradicate conditions where potential for high groundwater levels near the basement floor's elevation may exist. Experience has shown that trying to seal moisture out of a foundation is not nearly as effective as diverting the moisture with a drainage system before it gets inside the living space.

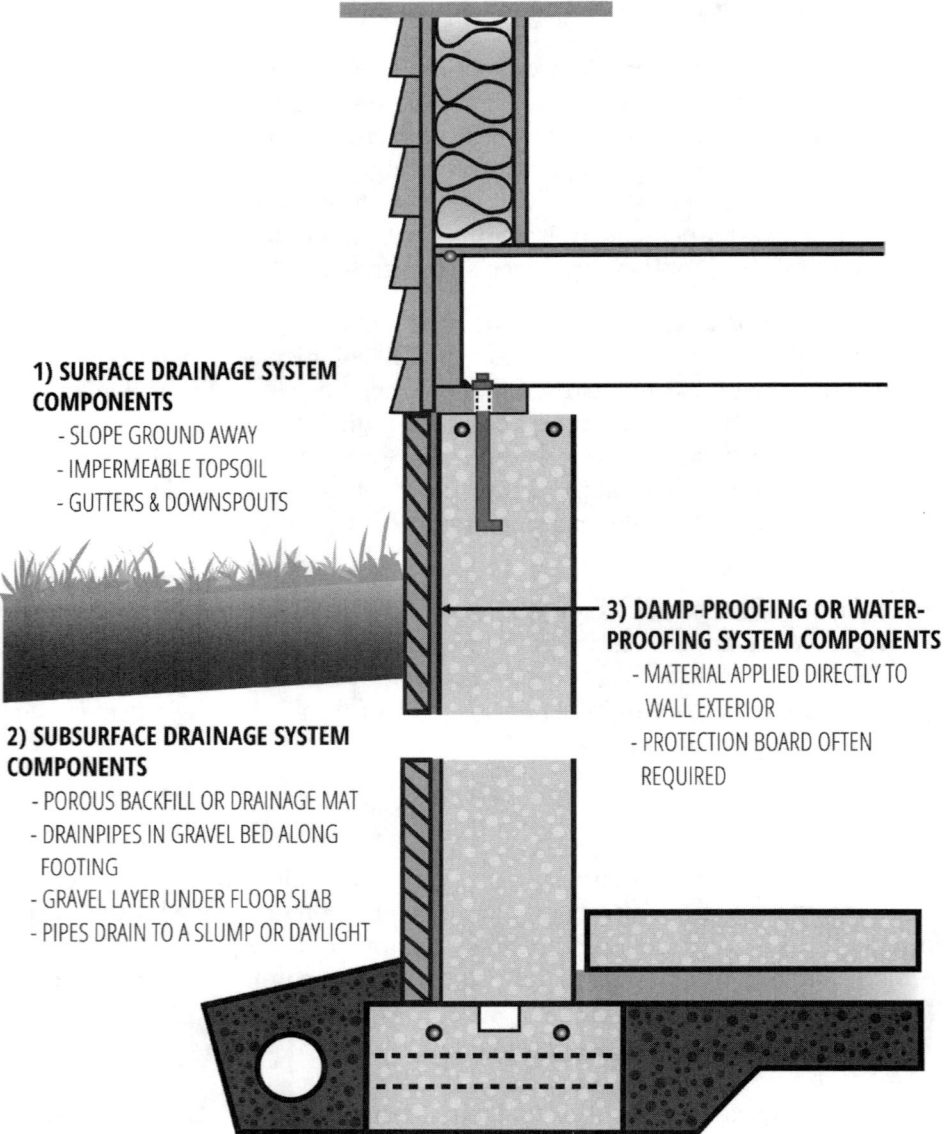

1) SURFACE DRAINAGE SYSTEM COMPONENTS
- SLOPE GROUND AWAY
- IMPERMEABLE TOPSOIL
- GUTTERS & DOWNSPOUTS

3) DAMP-PROOFING OR WATER-PROOFING SYSTEM COMPONENTS
- MATERIAL APPLIED DIRECTLY TO WALL EXTERIOR
- PROTECTION BOARD OFTEN REQUIRED

2) SUBSURFACE DRAINAGE SYSTEM COMPONENTS
- POROUS BACKFILL OR DRAINAGE MAT
- DRAINPIPES IN GRAVEL BED ALONG FOOTING
- GRAVEL LAYER UNDER FLOOR SLAB
- PIPES DRAIN TO A SLUMP OR DAYLIGHT

Waterproofing and Damp-Proofing

The terms "waterproofing" and "damp-proofing" both relate to moisture protection. However, they are often misapplied and incorrectly used by inspectors. The term "waterproofing" is often used when "damp-proofing" is more appropriate. Damp-proofing does not provide the same degree of moisture protection as does waterproofing.

Model building codes typically require damp-proofing of foundation walls that retain earth and enclose interior spaces and floors below grade. The damp-proofing shall be applied from the top of the footing to the finished grade.

Damp-proofing for masonry walls involves a Portland cement parging applied to the exterior of the wall. The parging shall be damp-proofed using one of the following materials:

- bituminous coating;
- acrylic-modified cement;
- surface-bonding cement;
- a permitted waterproofing material; or
- other approved methods or materials.

The use of waterproofing measures is reserved for conditions where a high water table or other severe soil-water conditions are known to exist. Strictly speaking, "waterproof" does not mean "watertight" (as with a boat hull). It simply involves the application of a more impermeable membrane on the foundation wall. With some exceptions, walls shall be waterproofed by one of the following methods:

- 2-ply hot-mopped felts;
- 55-pound roll roofing;
- 6-mil polyvinyl chloride (PVC);
- 6-mil polyethylene;
- 40-mil polymer-modified asphalt;
- 60-mil flexible polymer cement;
- 1/8-inch cement-based, fiber-reinforced waterproofing coating; or
- 60-mil, solvent-free, liquid-applied synthetic rubber.

Using 6-mil Poly for Waterproofing

The use of 6-mil poly as a waterproofing membrane on basement foundations helps to bridge small cracks and also minimizes the rate of moisture transport through the foundation wall by means of capillary action and vapor transmission. These sources of moisture transport add to moisture levels inside the basement and above-grade portions of the home. For these reasons, in an NAHB survey of foundation construction practices and moisture-related problems, basement walls with a 6-mil poly covering were 11 times less likely to experience leakage problems in comparison to typical damp-proofing practices (source: *Basement Water Leakage: Causes, Prevention, and Correction*; National Association of Home Builders, 1978).

The waterproofing method is recommended as a best practice, especially if the basement is intended to be used for storage or living space. Waterproofing could involve the simple application of damp-proofing, plus a layer of 6-mil poly on the exterior below-grade portions of a basement's foundation walls. Other single-ply or built-up membranes may also be used.

Damp-proofing is the application of one or more coatings of impervious compounds that prevent the passage of water vapor through walls under slight pressure.

Waterproofing is the application of a combination of sealing materials and impervious coatings to prevent the passage of moisture in either a vapor or liquid form under conditions of significant hydrostatic pressure.

Look for Foundation Cracks and Water

It is important to realize that all concrete and masonry construction will develop cracks due to the effects of shrinkage. As these cracks widen over time (usually due to small amounts of differential settlement in the soil supporting the foundation), the pathways for water intrusion through the foundation increase. Visible cracks may become a concern to homeowners even though these often have little relevance to the structural integrity of the foundation. The question becomes how to best control these cracks.

The optimum location for reinforcement to control cracking and prevent differential settlement is at the top and bottom of the foundation wall in a horizontal direction. Horizontal reinforcing of this type should be considered, in addition to adhering to code-required vertical reinforcement. By placing horizontal reinforcement, the wall acts as a deep beam, even after cracks initially form due to shrinkage during the concrete's curing process. If the wall is adequately tied (or doweled to the footing), then the reinforcement in the bottom of the wall may be placed horizontally along the length of the footing. The reinforcement at the top of the wall is known in masonry construction as a bond beam. Alternatively, truss-type reinforcing wire may also be used between horizontal courses of masonry block.

Epoxy Sealant for Masonry Cracks

An epoxy sealant can be injected into cracks in masonry foundation walls. Home inspectors often find cracks in poured concrete foundation walls. Typically, these cracks are shrinkage cracks and not an indication of major structural problems. The only problem other than the cosmetic appearance of shrinkage cracks in a poured concrete foundation wall is water penetration through those cracks. Epoxy sealant is an easy and relatively inexpensive solution for this potential moisture problem.

The process is simple. First, the crack is cleaned and exposed, and maybe even enlarged in some areas. A sealant is then applied over and along the crack. It serves as a barrier for the injection material, and also holds the injection nozzles in place so that no drilling of the foundation is necessary. The resin compound is a moisture-activated, flexible material that provides a permanent seal, even if there is future movement in the foundation. Next, the epoxy is injected. The epoxy is a two-part material consisting of resin and a hardener. When mixed, these liquids create a Super Glue®-like bond. Injecting a crack with epoxy resin is ideal in cracks where there will be little or no movement in the foundation.

Epoxy sealant can be applied at block foundation walls and at concrete floors of basements and garages.

Sealants for Through-Wall Penetrations

Utility penetrations through foundation walls should be carefully sealed on the exterior face of the wall prior to placement of waterproofing materials and backfill. High-quality urethane caulks are most suitable for this application. In addition, the wall construction should be inspected for penetrations due to voids or other problem areas (such as form ties) and appropriately repaired and sealed.

Cracking May Be the Result of Bad Practice

Good concrete construction practice is also important to minimize foundation cracking and porous concrete (voids) that will allow greater potential for foundation water intrusion. Good concreting practice includes use of an appropriate mix design (e.g. minimum 3,000-psi concrete), maintaining low water-to-cement ratio (minimize use of water to decrease concrete porosity), and vibrating concrete for good consolidation in forms.

Quiz #2

1. Roof system ventilation and insulation are important for a number of reasons: condensation control; temperature control; energy efficiency; and prevention of chronic _____-dam formation.

☐ water

☐ ice

☐ frost

☐ liquid

2. Roof _____ and projections provide a primary means of deflecting rainwater away from building walls.

☐ overhangs

☐ trees and bushes

☐ large gutters

☐ awnings

3. A(n) _____ is one layer of 15-pound asphalt felt applied over the studs or sheathing of all exterior walls.

☐ water-resistive barrier

☐ liquid-applied sealant

☐ REW

☐ EIFS barrier wall

4. T/F: Caulking of nail flanges (particularly at the window head and jambs) is critical to the prevention of moisture intrusion around commonly used nail-flange windows.

☐ True

☐ False

5. T/F: A drained-cavity WRE relies on deflection, drainage and drying to protect the wall from moisture damage.

☐ True

☐ False

6. _____ at exterior window and door openings shall extend to the surface of the exterior wall finish, or to the water-resistive barrier, for subsequent drainage.

☐ Flashing

☐ Sealant

☐ Fifteen-pound felt

☐ A 6-mil barrier

7. T/F: Approved corrosion-resistant flashings shall be installed continuously above all projecting wood trim.

    ☐ True

    ☐ False

8. T/F: In general, caulks and sealants should be relied on as the primary means of defense against water intrusion at joints in a WRE system.

    ☐ True

    ☐ False

9. T/F: Silicone rubber and urethane caulks generally give the best overall performance for exterior building envelope applications.

    ☐ True

    ☐ False

10. T/F: Model building standards typically require a minimum of 6-inch of fall in ground level over a distance of 10 feet from the perimeter of the building.

    ☐ True

    ☐ False

11. T/F: A condition that is beyond the scope of an inspector's consideration on a building site includes a high local water table (within 4 to 8 feet of the lowest proposed foundation floor/grade level).

    ☐ True

    ☐ False

12. T/F: Poor site drainage of surface water is perhaps the most important contributor to a foundation's moisture problems.

    ☐ True

    ☐ False

13. The upper layers of a _____ should be of moderate, low-permeability soil (with some clay content) to help reduce the direct infiltration of rainwater adjacent to the foundation.

    ☐ vinyl wallpaper

    ☐ stucco coating

    ☐ front-fill

    ☐ backfill

14. Generally speaking, current model building codes require that _____ be provided around all foundations that enclose habitable space (such as basements).

     ☐ drains

     ☐ gutters

     ☐ spikes

     ☐ swales

15. Model building codes typically require _____ of foundation walls that retain earth and enclose interior spaces and floors below grade.

     ☐ damp-proofing

     ☐ sealing

     ☐ coating

     ☐ waterproofing

16. _____ is the application of a combination of sealing materials and impervious coatings to prevent the passage of moisture in either a vapor or liquid form under conditions of significant hydrostatic pressure.

     ☐ Damp-proofing

     ☐ Waterproofing

     ☐ Draining

     ☐ Water-stacking

17. A(n) _____ sealant can be injected into cracks of masonry foundation walls to stop water intrusion.

     ☐ epoxy

     ☐ acrylic

     ☐ good

     ☐ gray-colored

Answer Key is on page 115.

Basement Wall Insulation

Basement wall finishes are exposed to a unique environment in terms of moisture concerns. The foremost concern is exterior moisture. This section focuses on the use of insulation, vapor barriers, and air-leakage sealing practices to construct finished basement areas.

The approaches for insulating and finishing basement spaces vary, depending on whether you're dealing with new or existing construction, and whether a basement is being only insulated but not finished. Existing basements obviously have limited options for using exterior foundation insulation. And some interior insulation approaches using foam that offer good moisture performance also require covering with a fire-resistant layer, such as gypsum, so they're a good choice for a finished basement, but not effective for only insulating an unfinished area.

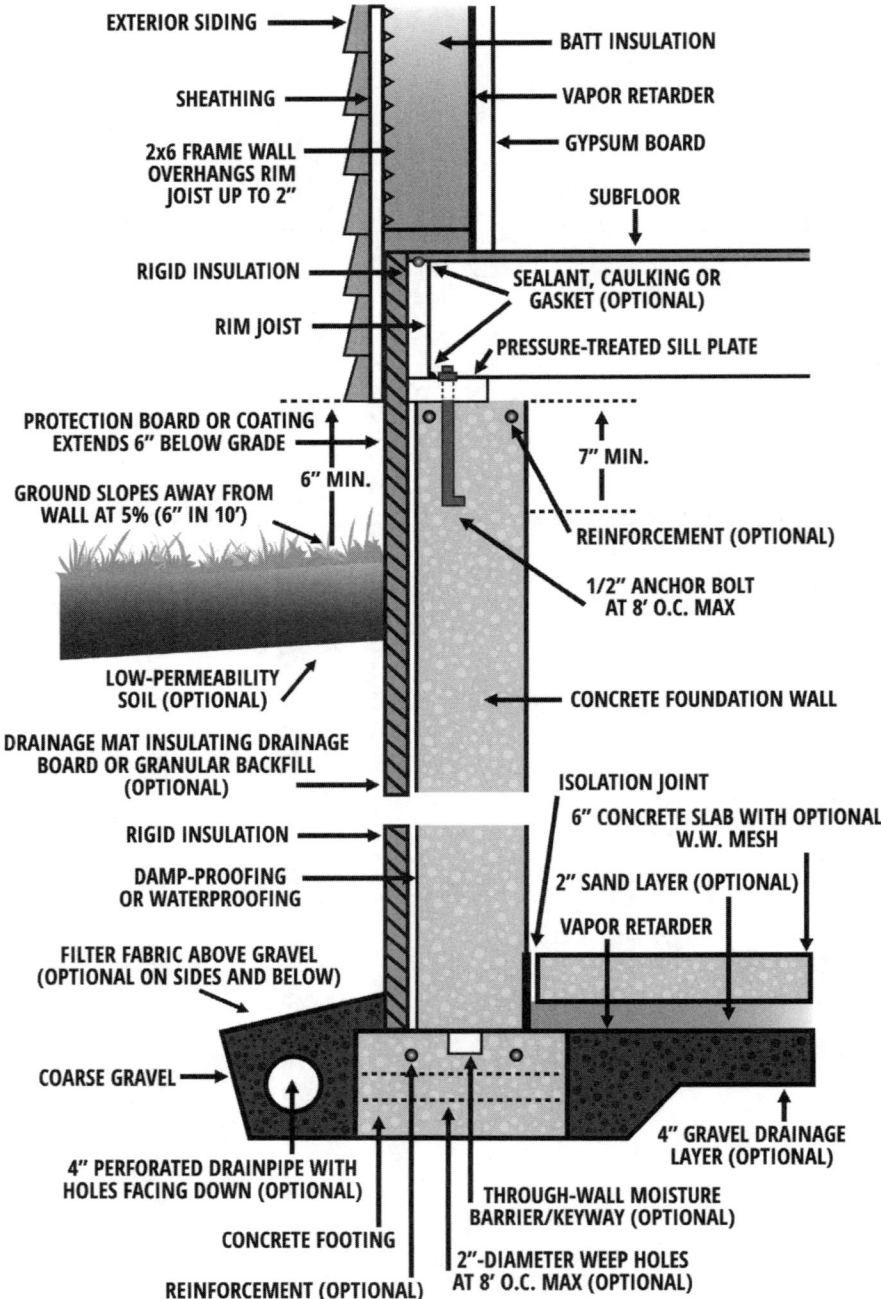

EXTERIOR SIDING

BATT INSULATION

SHEATHING

VAPOR RETARDER

2x6 FRAME WALL OVERHANGS RIM JOIST UP TO 2"

GYPSUM BOARD

SUBFLOOR

RIGID INSULATION

SEALANT, CAULKING OR GASKET (OPTIONAL)

RIM JOIST

PRESSURE-TREATED SILL PLATE

PROTECTION BOARD OR COATING EXTENDS 6" BELOW GRADE

6" MIN.

7" MIN.

GROUND SLOPES AWAY FROM WALL AT 5% (6" IN 10')

REINFORCEMENT (OPTIONAL)

1/2" ANCHOR BOLT AT 8' O.C. MAX

LOW-PERMEABILITY SOIL (OPTIONAL)

CONCRETE FOUNDATION WALL

DRAINAGE MAT INSULATING DRAINAGE BOARD OR GRANULAR BACKFILL (OPTIONAL)

ISOLATION JOINT

6" CONCRETE SLAB WITH OPTIONAL W.W. MESH

RIGID INSULATION

2" SAND LAYER (OPTIONAL)

DAMP-PROOFING OR WATERPROOFING

VAPOR RETARDER

FILTER FABRIC ABOVE GRAVEL (OPTIONAL ON SIDES AND BELOW)

COARSE GRAVEL

4" GRAVEL DRAINAGE LAYER (OPTIONAL)

4" PERFORATED DRAINPIPE WITH HOLES FACING DOWN (OPTIONAL)

THROUGH-WALL MOISTURE BARRIER/KEYWAY (OPTIONAL)

CONCRETE FOOTING

REINFORCEMENT (OPTIONAL)

2"-DIAMETER WEEP HOLES AT 8' O.C. MAX (OPTIONAL)

Strategies on basement finishing differ among various experts in the industry. Any successful basement finish design requires that exterior waterproofing, relative-humidity control in the basement, and air-sealing are all properly addressed.

Because inspectors work in both new and existing construction, the approach shown for basement insulating and finishing concentrates on interior insulation systems. Note that exterior insulation strategies using foam insulation panels on the outside of the foundation wall are also viable options for new construction, as these panels provide a moisture-tolerant insulation layer on the outside of the wall. This insulation layer moderates the temperature of the inside wall surface, and can also be integrated with exterior water- or damp-proofing. However, this approach requires shifting the house structure outward such that the sill plate overlaps the upper edge of the foundation insulation, protecting exterior insulation during construction, and providing long-term protection for the exposed insulation.

The illustration on the previous page depicts a concrete foundation wall with exterior insulation. The above-grade wood frame wall is constructed of 2x6s that overhang the foundation wall. The overhang can be up to 2 inches, but additional rigid insulation can be added that extends over the entire wall assembly. Another minor difference is that the figure shows a sand layer beneath the floor slab.

For interior insulation systems, the approaches offered are illustrated in the image on the following page. While this type of basement finish construction may be more commonly found in commercial applications for below-ground space, the concept is relatively new for residential construction as a best practice. Therefore, this strategy is included here primarily for consideration where traditional practices (e.g., the use of a warm-in-winter vapor retarder on the inside of the finish wall system) have resulted in moisture problems, and a wall system that dries toward the interior is desired. This technique, as well as traditional basement finish practices, is not intended to compensate for inadequate waterproofing, foundation drainage, indoor relative-humidity control, or air-leakage control.

Understanding How Basement Insulation and Finishes Should Dry to the Interior

Low-permeability and continuous vapor retarders on the interior side of basement finishes, such as polyethylene sheeting and vinyl wallpaper, should be avoided because they tend to trap moisture vapor moving through the foundation wall and slow the drying process for new foundations. Therefore, unfaced fiberglass batt insulation and permeable paint finishes on gypsum wallboard are preferred on basement finished-wall assemblies. Other proprietary basement finish systems using products such as rigid fiberglass insulating boards have also performed well in testing and use. However, the use of certified installers may be required by the manufacturer.

Finding Semi-Permeable Rigid Foam Insulation Between the Foundation Wall and Finish-Wall Assembly

The use of rigid foam creates a buffer of moisture-resistant material between the finish-wall materials and the basement foundation wall. Because below-grade portions of the foundation wall must be able to dry to the interior, semi-permeable, rigid-foam insulating sheathing products, such as EPS or XPS, should be used. Since product-permeability levels vary by manufacturer, the product specifications of the perm rating for the required thickness should be greater than 1 perm.

Finding Interior Foam Insulation and a Fire Hazard

The use of semi-permeable rigid foam insulation on the inside of basement foundation walls is often found during an inspection of the foundation of the house. It is a good strategy for a moisture-resistant finished basement. However, fire and smoke characteristics of this type of insulation will require that it be covered with a fire-resistant layer like gypsum. This works fine when the basement is being finished. But if a basement will only be insulated and not finished, a fire-rated foam panel or similar fire-rated covering needs to be used. Because the above-grade portions of the basement wall can dry to the outside, fire-rated insulation on these surfaces can be impermeable (e.g., it can have a foil facing). But insulating approaches that restrict the drying potential of below-grade portions of the foundation wall toward the outside should be avoided. Joints in the foam sheathings should be taped and sealed. If additional insulation is required or desired, a frame wall may be built and cavity insulation installed, as shown in the following image.

Check for Warm, Humid Indoor Basement Air Leaking Through the Finish

To prevent humid interior basement air from leaking into the finished-wall assembly and then condensing, the interior side of the assembly should be sealed against air leakage. The ideal approach uses the gypsum wallboard as an air barrier, and requires sealing any penetrations through or leaks around the panels. Air-sealing of ceiling penetrations in the basement should also be addressed. This approach is called the "airtight drywall approach." Also, joints in the foam insulation should be taped and sealed.

Check for Moisture at the Bottom of the Basement's Finished Walls

Gypsum wallboard, wood trim and wood framing will wick moisture from the slab. In addition, the slab will tend to cool materials that it is in contact with, creating higher surface humidity levels that may support mold growth. Therefore, finishes and baseboard trim should be held up about 1/2-inch from the slab surface. This gap could be sealed with caulk or sealant to prevent air leakage from indoors into the wall assembly. In addition, a thin foam-plastic sill sealer may be used underneath the finished wall's bottom plate for added moisture protection. During the inspection of the basement, check the bottom of the finished wall for moisture.

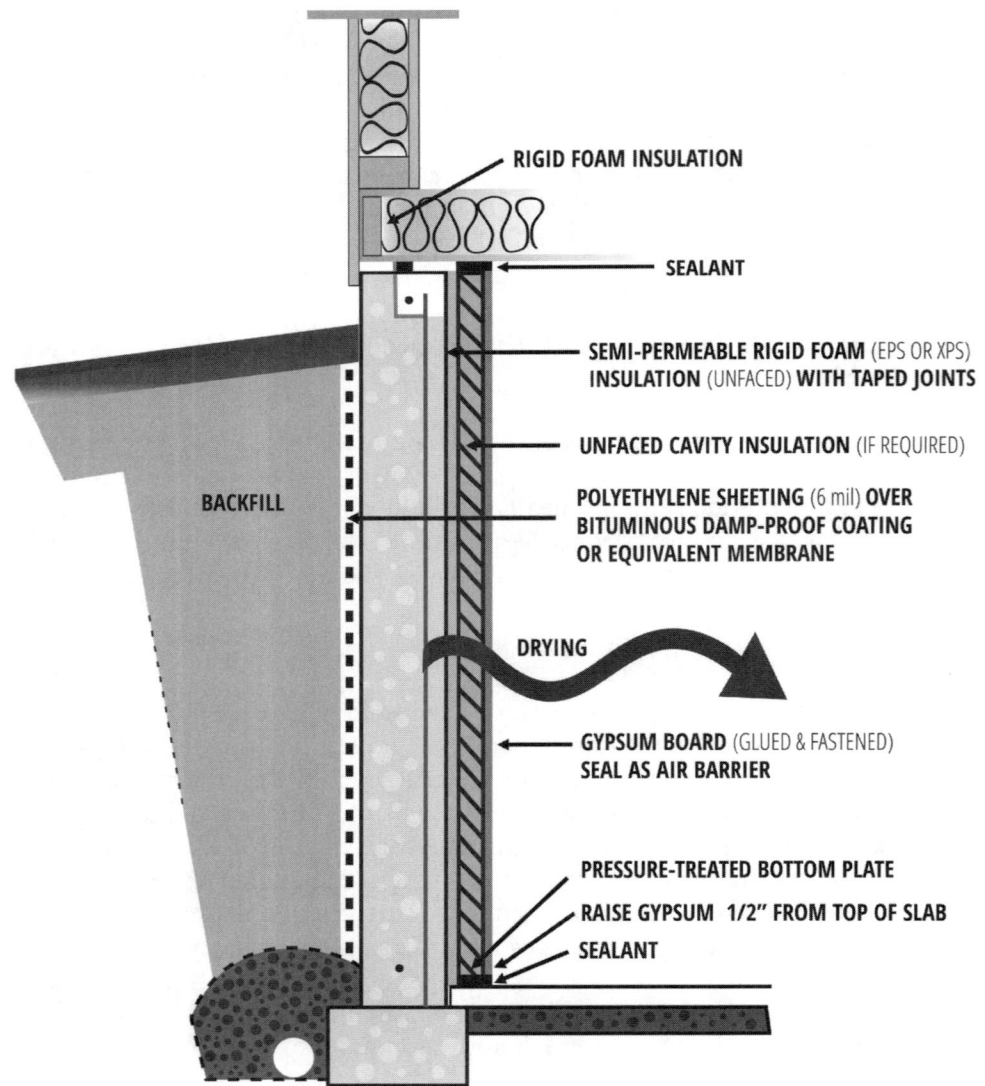

Slab-on-Grade Construction

Let's learn about moisture and slab-on-grade foundation construction. Slab-on-grade construction includes thickened-edge or monolithic slab foundation construction. Given their similarity, concrete or masonry stem-wall foundations with an independent above-grade slab floor will be discussed. Moisture-resistant installations are summarized in the image on the following page. They are relatively simple in comparison to the requirements for basement construction; however, many of the same principles apply. Slabs below the outside ground level, as with partial or full-basement construction, should be built in accordance with basement foundation recommendations. Moisture-resistant concrete floor finishes are also addressed.

Slab-on-grade construction is most suitable for relatively flat sites. However, for sites that are low-lying and flat, surface-water ponding may occur seasonally or with rainfall events. On those types of sites, a crawlspace may be found. Appropriate moisture-resistant site design and foundation installation should be checked during an inspection. In mixed and cold climates, pay careful attention to the slab edge or foundation perimeter insulation to determine whether they avoid thermal bridges, which can cause cold slab surfaces and condensation. As mentioned before, a typical home inspection will not necessarily go into great detail about site design and the builder's methods and practices in relation to moisture-resistant foundations. However, a good understanding of the best practices for moisture-resistant construction will greatly improve the inspector's ability to search for and diagnose moisture problems.

Is the Foundation Pad on a Mound with Clearance?

The elevation of a slab-on-grade foundation (a thickened-edge slab or independent slab and stem-wall foundation) should be a minimum of 8 inches above the exterior finish grade.

In areas with heavy rainfall, clearances greater than 8 inches or other rain-control measures, such as back-vented cladding with an ice and water shield 18 inches up the wall, may be more desirable. The foundation elevation to achieve this effect must be coordinated with the site plan. In particular, topsoil must be removed and the foundation pad must be built up with suitable (compactible) structural fill material, as required. Fills of more than 12 inches thick are generally required to be engineered. As a simple test, the slab foundation pad should be able to support a loaded dump truck with minimal depression from the wheel load (1/2-inch or less). With a properly mounded slab and site grading, surface water will drain away and minimize the moisture load around and beneath the slab.

The Required Vapor Retarder with a Capillary Break Beneath It

A vapor barrier (6-mil poly or equal) or approved vapor retarder is generally required below any slab intended as a floor for habitable space. The joints should be lapped not less than 6 inches. It should be placed in direct contact with the underside of the concrete slab. The vapor barrier will prevent moisture vapor from adding to the building's interior moisture load, and also serves as a break to the capillary movement of moisture.

A capillary-break layer — generally, 4 inches of clean graded sand, gravel, crushed stone or crushed blast-furnace slag — further prevents bulk soil moisture from wicking up to the bottom of the slab. Building codes typically require a capillary layer below the slab, and this should be provided under the vapor barrier so that water cannot be trapped in a gravel layer between the vapor barrier and the slab. The vapor barrier will help to cure the concrete properly if it is properly damp-cured on the top surface by preventing exposure to excessive drying conditions, and if excessive water in the concrete mix is avoided. If workability of the concrete is a concern, use a mix designed with additives, such as plasticizers, which will eliminate the need for additional water.

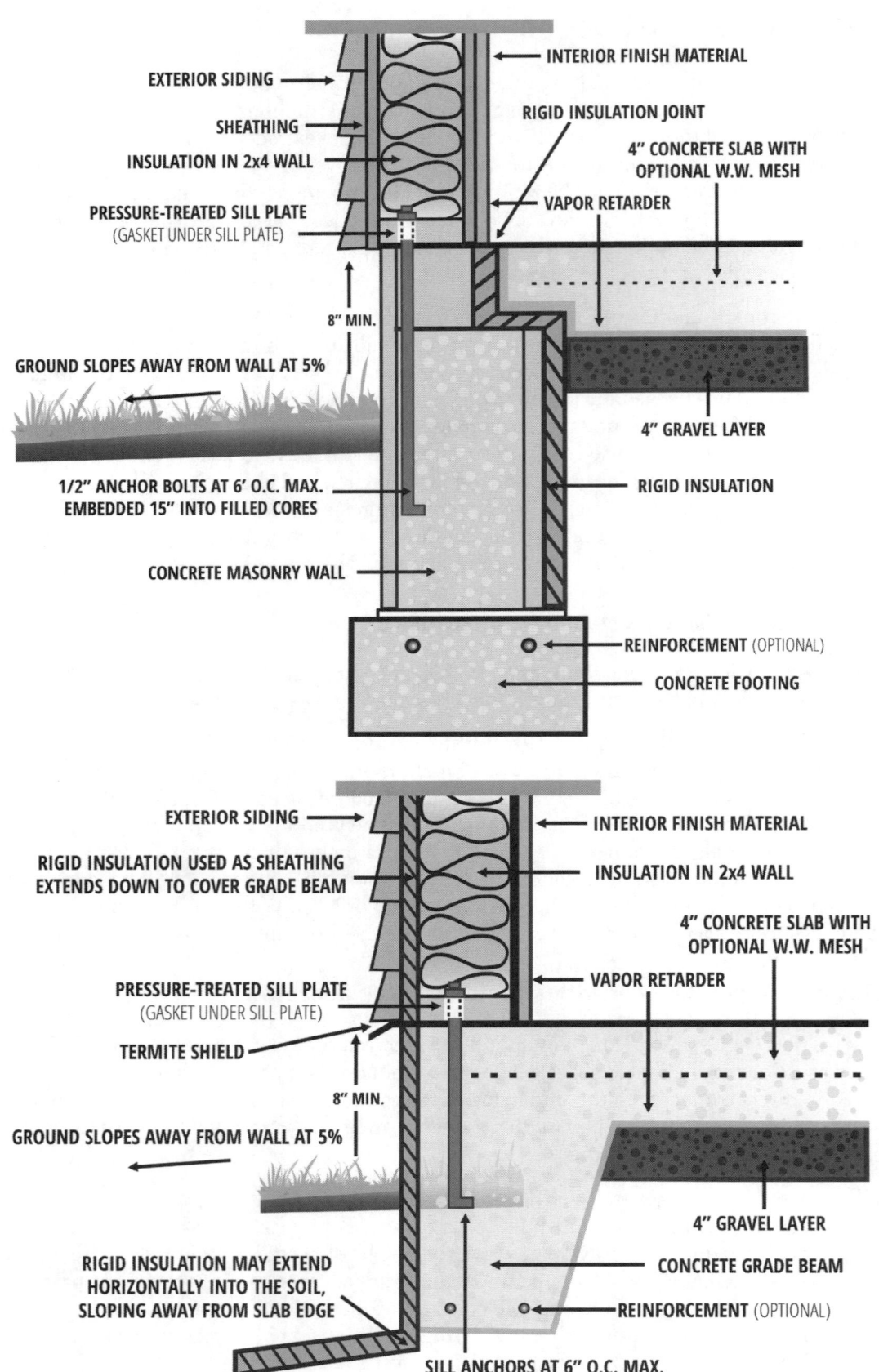

EXTERIOR SIDING

SHEATHING

INSULATION IN 2x4 WALL

PRESSURE-TREATED SILL PLATE
(GASKET UNDER SILL PLATE)

8" MIN.

GROUND SLOPES AWAY FROM WALL AT 5%

1/2" ANCHOR BOLTS AT 6' O.C. MAX.
EMBEDDED 15" INTO FILLED CORES

CONCRETE MASONRY WALL

INTERIOR FINISH MATERIAL

RIGID INSULATION JOINT

4" CONCRETE SLAB WITH
OPTIONAL W.W. MESH

VAPOR RETARDER

4" GRAVEL LAYER

RIGID INSULATION

REINFORCEMENT (OPTIONAL)

CONCRETE FOOTING

EXTERIOR SIDING

RIGID INSULATION USED AS SHEATHING
EXTENDS DOWN TO COVER GRADE BEAM

PRESSURE-TREATED SILL PLATE
(GASKET UNDER SILL PLATE)

TERMITE SHIELD

8" MIN.

GROUND SLOPES AWAY FROM WALL AT 5%

RIGID INSULATION MAY EXTEND
HORIZONTALLY INTO THE SOIL,
SLOPING AWAY FROM SLAB EDGE

INTERIOR FINISH MATERIAL

INSULATION IN 2x4 WALL

4" CONCRETE SLAB WITH
OPTIONAL W.W. MESH

VAPOR RETARDER

4" GRAVEL LAYER

CONCRETE GRADE BEAM

REINFORCEMENT (OPTIONAL)

SILL ANCHORS AT 6" O.C. MAX.

Cracks in the Slab and Moisture Problems

Concrete will crack as a normal outcome of the curing process. Cracking can be worsened if uneven bearing conditions, such as un-compacted fill areas, exist under the slab.

The use of welded-wire fabric reinforcement provides a means of controlling the severity of cracking. While fiber-reinforced concrete may also provide adequate crack control, the introduction of fibers may tend to decrease the workability of wet concrete. Therefore, the appropriate concrete-mix design and placement should be considered with the use of fiber-reinforced concrete to prevent problems created by use of additional water to improve workability.

Excessive use of water for workability will tend to allow moisture to more readily penetrate the concrete slab, weaken the concrete, and lead to differential drying issues and cracking. Excessive cracking can allow additional moisture, as well as radon gas, to penetrate more easily through the slab.

Concrete control joints may also be used to control random cracking by creating planned lines of weakness in the slab. Shrinkage and curing cracks generally occur in any continuous length of concrete greater than about 12 feet.

Rebar Reduces Cracking

As with basement foundations and footings, the local building code may not require horizontal reinforcement of the thickened-edge footing of a monolithic slab on grade. The same applies to stem-wall and independent slab construction.

However, the information in this guide describes a minimum of a continuous #5 rebar located horizontally at the top and bottom of the thickened edge of a monolithic slab or stem wall. This allows the thickened slab-edge (the footing) to act as a moderately reinforced grade beam to reduce cracking from differential settlement. Concrete and masonry stem walls may be reinforced with horizontal reinforcement bars in a manner similar to that recommended for basement walls. For difficult site-soil conditions, such as expansive or weak soils, other types of concrete slab foundations may be required or advisable, such as mat foundations or post-tensioned slabs.

Insulation on the Exterior Slab-on-Grade Foundations May Be Found

Building codes allow foundation insulation to be placed in various locations at the perimeter of a slab-on-grade foundation. Ideally, the best location for insulation in slab-on-grade foundations is on the vertical, outside face of the foundation. In this location, thermal bridges are minimized, energy efficiency is maximized, and the slab's surface temperature is moderated to prevent the risk of condensation during cold weather. If slab-on-grade insulation is placed in a different location (such as on the inside face of the perimeter foundation wall), then care should be taken to create a continuous thermal break between the indoor portions of the slab and the exterior.

When used, exterior foundation insulation must be protected from the elements at additional expense. One way a builder can reduce costs while using exterior-slab perimeter insulation is to use a frost-protected shallow foundation. These foundations are found in North America. They are most cost-effective in climates where required frost depths are substantially greater than 12 inches and foundation insulation requirements are more stringent.

Frost-Protected Shallow Foundations

Frost-protected shallow foundation (FPSF) systems offer a design option that allows for shallower footing depths by raising the frost depth around the building through the use of insulation. FPSF systems offer many advantages for slab-on-grade construction in cold climates, including:

- reduced construction cost;
- increased energy efficiency;
- improved slab comfort; and
- increased slab temperatures to prevent condensation.

Ideally, heated slab systems may be used with insulation amounts increased above that minimally required for FPSFs.

Slab-on-Grade Insulation and Finishes

Like basement wall finishes, finishes on concrete floor slabs on grade are exposed to a unique environment due to direct ground contact. This section of the book talks about what to look for when inspecting a moisture-resistant floor finish on a concrete slab on grade.

Moisture-Resistant Finishes May Be Installed

From a moisture perspective, tile, terrazzo, stained decorative concrete, and other moisture-resistant finishes are ideal for slab-on-grade construction. These materials are resistant to flooding and other sources of moisture damage, and are typical in southern and hot and humid climates. In such cases, the primary concerns are limiting indoor humidity, providing a sub-slab vapor barrier directly below the concrete slab (such 6-mil polyethylene), and providing a capillary break (such as a 3- to 4-inch thick clean gravel layer).

Slab Insulation Should Be Installed with Moisture-Sensitive Finishes

Carpet and wood-based floor finishes should not be applied directly to slabs on grade unless the slab or finish surface temperature is raised near room temperature. Moderated floor temperatures that can accommodate moisture-sensitive finishes can be achieved with sub-slab or slab-surface insulation, as well as perimeter insulation, to prevent thermal short-circuits in the slab. Where slab temperatures are chilled by cold, outdoor winter conditions, or cooled by ground temperatures during the spring and summer, surface condensation or high humidity may result in mold growth or condensation damage.

Missing Slab Insulation

Slabs that do not have a moisture-vapor barrier underneath often are not suitable for finished flooring in living spaces. This can be the case in both slab-on-grade foundations and for basement slabs. Newer model building codes require a moisture vapor barrier (e.g., 6-mil poly) underneath slab-on-grade floors serving living spaces. In the event that this requirement is not met in an existing slab on grade or basement slab, water vapor must be controlled from the top of the slab surface. See the image on the next page.

Signs of Moisture Problems

If a slab shows signs of a pre-existing moisture problem, such as dampness or condensation, salt deposition, or standing water, the issue should be addressed before moving ahead with finish flooring. Once any pre-existing moisture issues with the slab are addressed, a floor-finish assembly that can accommodate a small amount of upward moisture flow can be installed. One viable approach involves the use of a rigid, semi-permeable insulating sheathing (greater than 1 perm), such as extruded polystyrene on top of the slab, with 12- to 16-inch on-center furring above the foam, followed by a layer of tongue-and-groove plywood for the subfloor. The finish flooring above the plywood should be a breathable finish, so impermeable materials, such as vinyl flooring, should be avoided. With this type of assembly installed, a relatively dry slab without a sub-slab layer of poly can be finished and designed to accommodate a limited amount of moisture that dries upward (see bottom detail in the image below).

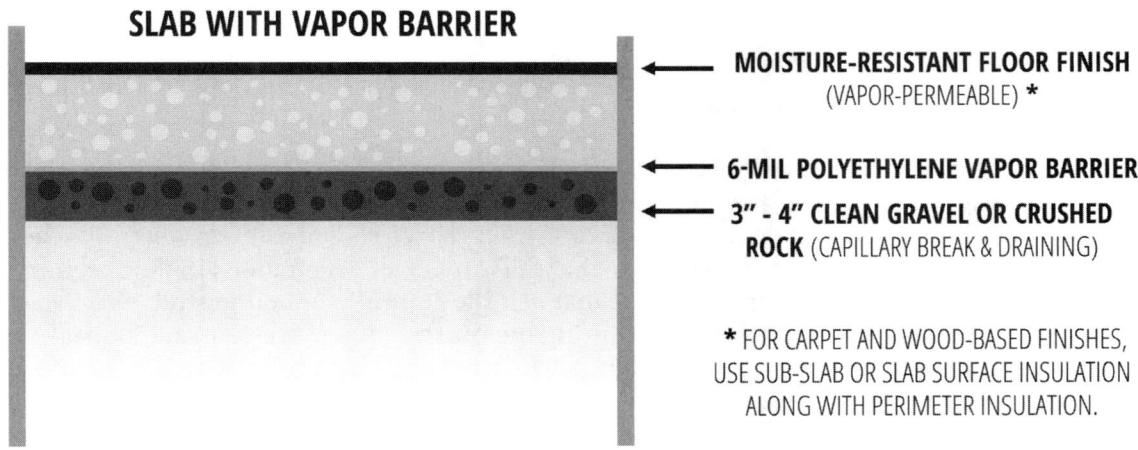

SLAB WITH VAPOR BARRIER

← **MOISTURE-RESISTANT FLOOR FINISH**
(VAPOR-PERMEABLE) *

← **6-MIL POLYETHYLENE VAPOR BARRIER**

← **3" - 4" CLEAN GRAVEL OR CRUSHED ROCK** (CAPILLARY BREAK & DRAINING)

* FOR CARPET AND WOOD-BASED FINISHES, USE SUB-SLAB OR SLAB SURFACE INSULATION ALONG WITH PERIMETER INSULATION.

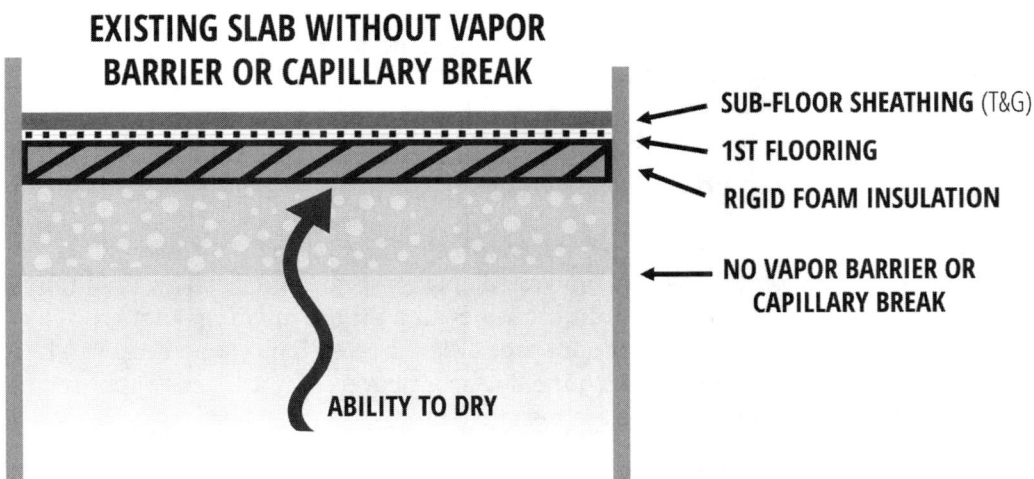

EXISTING SLAB WITHOUT VAPOR BARRIER OR CAPILLARY BREAK

← **SUB-FLOOR SHEATHING** (T&G)

← **1ST FLOORING**

← **RIGID FOAM INSULATION**

← **NO VAPOR BARRIER OR CAPILLARY BREAK**

ABILITY TO DRY

Crawlspaces and Moisture

The top causes of moisture problems in crawlspaces include poor site drainage, lack of a ground vapor barrier, and crawlspace ventilation during humid summer conditions. Crawlspace moisture damage and mold formation can be caused by any one of these issues. Therefore, they must be addressed for moisture-resistant crawlspace foundations.

Crawlspace construction should ideally result in an interior crawlspace ground surface that is at or above the exterior finish grade. That is not often the case. Extra attention is required for foundation drainage for crawlspaces below the exterior finish grade. Also, venting crawlspaces in humid conditions can result in condensation of warm, moist air on cool surfaces in the crawlspace, including ductwork, and the underside of floor framing. In very humid conditions, this can lead to water accumulation, wet insulation, material degradation, and mold.

Use of a Mud Slab

Groundcover laid on crawlspace floors can become damaged or disturbed over time, resulting in lost effectiveness. In addition, it is difficult to drain a groundcover that might become wetted on the top surface occasionally, such as from a plumbing leak. As an enhancement that further emulates conventional basement construction, a mud slab (e.g. 2-inch-thick concrete slab) may be placed on top of the groundcover and modestly sloped to drain to a sump pit, if required for low-lying, flood-prone, or otherwise wet sites.

Check for Groundcover at the Crawlspace

As a best practice, all exposed earth (dirt) on a crawlspace floor should be covered by a vapor retarder in the form of a minimum 6-mil layer of polyethylene sheeting. The joints of the vapor retarder should overlap 6 inches and should be sealed or taped. The edges should extend at least 6 inches up the wall and should be secured and sealed to the walls and to all penetrations in the sheeting with tape or adhesive. This is a simple measure that helps to control ground moisture effectively. If the groundcover initially installed is damaged during the construction process, an additional layer should be added, or damaged sections should be patched and sealed.

Check Drainage and Damp-Proofing for Crawlspaces Below the Exterior Grade

If the crawlspace elevation is below the exterior finish grade, foundation drainage and foundation wall damp-proofing (such as bituminous coating on the below-grade exterior face of the crawlspace's foundation wall) should be provided in a fashion similar to that required for basements. Crawlspaces of this type should use the damp-proofing and the exterior drainage system noted earlier for basements.

Evaluate Vented and Non-Vented Crawlspaces

There are essentially two choices for ventilation of crawlspaces. The first follows conventional ventilation practices, and the second follows a non-vented crawlspace design strategy. Traditional crawlspace ventilation requirements call for a minimum net area for the openings that are at least 1 square foot for each 150 square feet of under-floor space area. The ventilation openings can be reduced from 1:150 to 1:1,500 where the earth/ground surface is covered by a Class I vapor retarder (0.1 perm or less) and the ventilation openings are installed.

Vents should be placed on at least two opposing sides of the foundation and as close as practical to the corners of the foundation, and as high as possible on the foundation walls. This method is very well-established, but the inspector should refer to the locally applicable building code before recording evaluations.

A second option reflects mounting evidence, as well as recognition of recent model building codes, that non-vented crawlspaces are an acceptable method of crawlspace foundation construction. The method is particularly suitable for hot and humid climates where ventilating with outdoor air actually adds moisture to the crawlspace during much of the year, and should be considered as an option in other climates. However, there's more to it than simply taking out the vents.

The following factors should be known by the inspector when inspecting an unvented crawlspace:

- functional exterior grading and site drainage;
- air leakage between the outdoors and the crawlspace area (mainly at the top of the foundation wall and the building floor perimeter);
- insulation on the interior of the crawlspace's perimeter walls (not the floor above), such as 2 inches of rigid foam insulation;
- the use of 6-mil polyethylene groundcover in the crawlspace, with joints lapped and sealed (always recommended in this guide);
- damp-proofing of the foundation walls, and the installation of an exterior drainage system if the crawlspace's ground elevation is lower than the outside finish grade; and
- some ventilation of the crawlspace with conditioned air.

Recent model building codes also require that the non-vented crawlspace be treated as a conditioned basement space — that is, it's supplied with conditioned air, along with a return-air transfer grille placed in the floor above the crawlspace. Alternatively, the crawlspace must be mechanically ventilated or designed as an under-floor space plenum for the distribution of conditioned air. While non-vented crawlspace designs without these features have performed well, inspectors should check with local code requirements when inspecting a non-vented crawlspace.

Understanding Vented vs. Unvented Crawlspaces

The principal perceived advantage of a vented crawlspace over an unvented one is that venting can minimize radon and moisture-related decay hazards by diluting the crawlspace air. Venting can complement other moisture- and radon-control measures, such as groundcover and proper drainage. However, although increased air flow in the crawlspace may offer some dilution potential for ground-source moisture and radon, it will not necessarily solve a serious problem.

The principal disadvantages of a vented crawlspace over an unvented one are:

- pipes and ducts must be insulated against heat loss and freezing;
- usually, a larger area must be insulated, which may increase the cost; and
- in some climates, warm, humid air circulated into the cool crawlspace can actually cause excessive moisture levels in wood.

Vented crawlspaces are often provided with operable vents that can be closed to reduce winter heat losses, but may also potentially increase radon infiltration. Although not their original purpose, the vents can also be closed in summer to keep out moist exterior air that can have a dew point above the crawlspace's temperature.

It is not necessary to vent a crawlspace for moisture control if it is open to an adjacent basement, and venting is clearly incompatible with crawlspaces used as heat-distribution plenums. In fact, there are several advantages to designing crawlspaces as semi-heated zones. Duct and pipe insulation can be reduced, and the foundation can be insulated at the crawlspace perimeter instead of its ceiling. This usually requires less insulation, simplifies installation difficulties in some cases, and can be detailed to minimize condensation hazards.

Although unvented crawlspaces have been recommended "except under severe moisture conditions," according to the University of Illinois's Small Homes Council, moisture problems in crawlspaces are common enough that many agencies are unwilling to endorse closing the vents year-round.

Soil type and the groundwater level are key factors influencing moisture conditions. It should be acknowledged that a crawlspace can be designed as a short basement (with a slurry slab floor), and, having a higher floor level, is subject to less moisture, in most cases. Viewed in this way, the main distinction between unvented crawlspaces and basements is in the owner's accessibility and the likelihood of noticing moisture problems.

Frost-Protected Shallow Foundation Using Non-Vented Crawlspace

With a non-vented crawlspace, a frost-protected shallow foundation strategy provides for energy efficiency, as well as cost-effective foundation construction in areas where frost depths exceed about 24 inches. The inspector is referred to the information on this foundation technology found in the section on slab foundation construction.

Quiz #3

1. T/F: Any successful basement finish design requires that exterior waterproofing, relative humidity control in the basement, and air-sealing are properly addressed.

 ☐ True
 ☐ False

2. For some climates, low-permeability and continuous vapor retarders on the _____ side of basement finishes, such as polyethylene sheeting or vinyl wallpaper, should be avoided because they tend to trap moisture vapor moving through the foundation.

 ☐ surface
 ☐ upper
 ☐ lower
 ☐ interior

3. T/F: The fire and smoke characteristics of semi-permeable, rigid foam insulation on the inside of a basement foundation wall require that it be covered with a fire-resistant layer, such as gypsum.

 ☐ True
 ☐ False

4. If significant interior air leaks into an attic, _____ may not be sufficient to prevent moisture and condensation problems in the attic.

 ☐ insulation baffles
 ☐ ventilation
 ☐ sheathing
 ☐ the structure

5. T/F: In finished basements, finishes and baseboard trim should be held up about 1/2-inch from the slab surface.

 ☐ True
 ☐ False

6. The elevation of a slab-on-grade foundation (thickened-edge slab or independent slab and stem-wall foundation) should be a minimum of _____ above the exterior finish grade.

 ☐ 8 inches
 ☐ 1 inch
 ☐ 12 inches

7. A vapor barrier (such as 6-mil poly) or other approved _____ is generally required, by standards, below any slab intended as a floor for habitable space.

    ☐ gravel layer
    ☐ vapor retarder
    ☐ drainage
    ☐ sand

8. T/F: Ideally, the best location for insulation in slab-on-grade foundations is on the vertical, outside face of the foundation.

    ☐ True
    ☐ False

9. T/F: Carpet and wood-based floor finishes should not be applied directly to slabs on grade unless the slab or finish surface temperature is raised near room temperature.

    ☐ True
    ☐ False

10. T/F: If a basement concrete floor slab shows signs of a pre-existing moisture problem, such as dampness or condensation, salt deposition, or standing water, the issue should be addressed after installing the finish flooring.

    ☐ True
    ☐ False

11. The top causes of moisture problems in crawlspaces include poor _____ drainage, lack of a ground vapor _____, and crawlspace ventilation during humid summer conditions.

    ☐ sewer..... barrier
    ☐ site..... intrusion
    ☐ driveway..... retention
    ☐ site..... barrier

12. T/F: If the crawlspace elevation is below the exterior finish grade, foundation drainage and foundation wall damp-proofing should be provided in a fashion similar to that required for basements.

    ☐ True
    ☐ False

13. T/F: It is not necessary to vent a crawlspace for moisture control if it is open to an adjacent basement.

    ☐ True
    ☐ False

Answer Key is on page 116.

Checking Ground Clearances

Checking Ground Clearances for Wood Protection

Decay of common wood framing materials can begin when the moisture content of untreated wood exceeds 20%. In foundation and building applications, these conditions should be avoided by adherence to minimum ground clearances and detailing requirements.

The ground clearances outlined in this section are considered minimums that have worked reasonably well in typical climates. In climates with frequent rainfall, or for sites with continuously moist ground conditions, greater clearances are recommended. In addition, capillary breaks are important, particularly when clearances are at minimums. Capillary breaks help to protect wood from wicking up moisture around the foundation from the ground. Capillary breaks may be in the form of materials such as metal flashing, tarred felt paper, sill-sealer foam stripping, and polyethylene. When wood has direct ground contact, or if clearances are less than those required, then preservative-treated wood or other moisture-resistant materials should be used.

CRAWLSPACE PIER

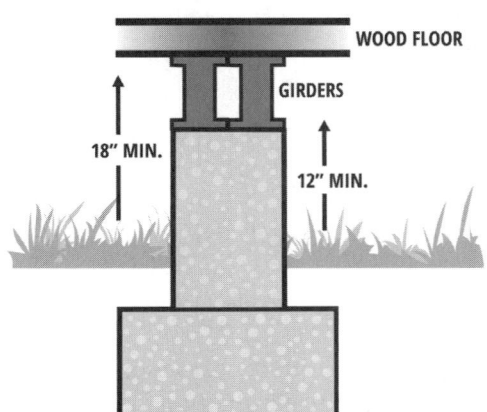

COLUMN SUPPORT

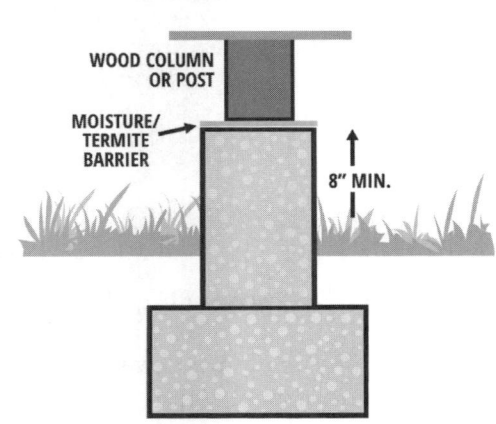

BEAM POCKET

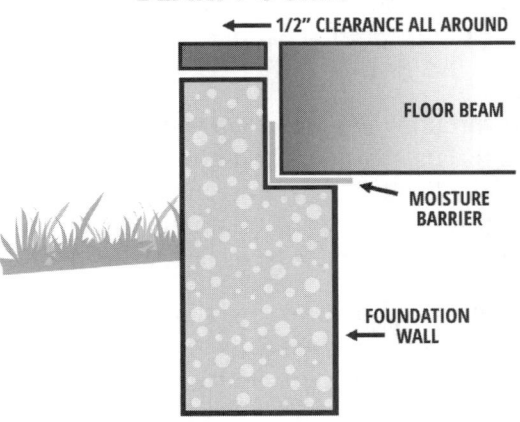

CLEARANCE FROM EXTERIOR GRADE

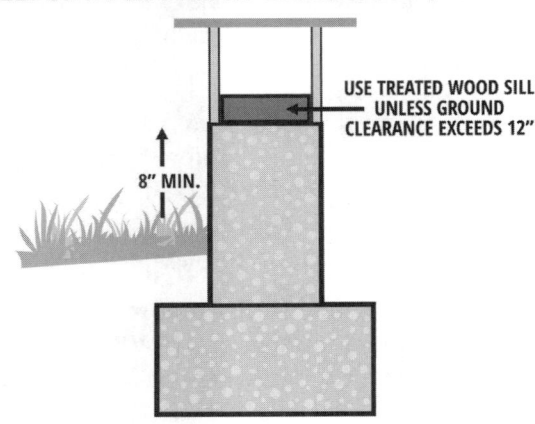

Check for an 8-inch Minimum Clearance

One of the oldest and most trustworthy practices to use to prevent wood and other moisture-sensitive materials from decaying is to install a separation from the constant uptake of moisture from the ground. Decay conditions can occur when wood is in direct ground contact, or when moisture wicks through other materials, such as concrete or masonry. Some details for popular methods used to separate wood from ground moisture are shown in the image on the previous page.

Most building codes require a 6-inch minimum clearance between untreated wood and the exterior grade, and some codes allow a 2-inch reduction in this clearance if brick veneer separates internal wood materials from the exterior grade. A minimum of 8 inches of clearance between untreated wood and the exterior ground level is recommended by many experienced building inspectors. In other conditions shown in the previous image, ground clearance recommendations vary. For example, floor beams in crawlspaces are required to have a 12-inch minimum clearance to the interior grade as much for reasons of access as for moisture protection.

Use of Foam Sill Sealer Strip on Foundation Sill and Wall Sole Plates

Wood sill plates or wall sole plates on exterior foundation walls can be exposed to moisture due to wicking through concrete (capillary action) or due to condensation. Using a foam sill sealer product (e.g., 1/8-inch-thick closed-cell foam strip) creates a capillary break as well as a modest thermal break. It also prevents a common air-leakage path that can contribute to moisture vapor transport and condensation.

Checking Wood Preservative

When Wood Needs to Be Preservative-Treated

There are often situations where wood cannot be adequately separated from ground moisture or protected from exterior moisture sources. In these situations, either naturally decay-resistant wood or preservative-treated wood must be used. In some cases, wood alternatives may be considered, such as plastic porch posts with metal pipe inserts, plastic decking, concrete posts or piers, or plastic lumber composites. The focus of this section is on identifying proper specifications and use of preservative-treated wood to ensure moisture (decay) resistance and durable performance. The recommendations in this section are based on the standards and recommendations of the Southern Pine Council and the American Wood Preservers Association (AWPA).

In recent years, changes have occurred in the availability of certain wood-preservative treatment chemicals for use in residential projects. Therefore, it is important to understand how these changes affect treatment requirements for various types of wood and applications. In particular, the use of CCA (chromated copper arsenate) has been discontinued as a wood treatment except in certain commercial and agricultural applications (for pile foundations, fence posts, etc.).

However, there are exceptions. For example, CCA-treated lumber and plywood are still available for use in permanent wood foundations (PWFs) in residential as well as commercial and agricultural applications. For most residential applications, however, newer forms of treatment are the only choices.

It's important to realize that many of the newer lumber preservative treatments may increase the corrosion rate of galvanized fasteners by a factor of 2 or 3, under standardized test conditions. Therefore, in cases of exposure to moisture at decks, porches and balconies, it is recommended that stainless steel fasteners and connector materials be considered.

At a minimum, hot-dipped galvanization or a G120 galvanic coating should be specified for steel fasteners and cold-formed steel connectors. A G120 coating provides at least twice the galvanic coating commonly used for framing connectors in residential construction. Connectors within the building envelope that are in contact with newer lumber preservative treatments are generally exempted, such as 1/2-inch-diameter sill anchor bolts.

Treated Wood Applications

Table 10 - Use Categories for Treated Softwood Lumber and Plywood			
Use Category	**Service Conditions**	**Typical Applications**	**Types of Protection**
UC1	Dry (interior & above ground)	Interior construction and furnishings	Insects only
UC2	Dry (interior above ground)	Interior construction	Decay and insects
UC3A	Periodic wetting (above ground)	Coated millwork, siding and trim	Decay and insects
UC3B	Prolonged wetting (above ground)	Decking, deck joists, fence pickets, sill plates, uncoated millwork	Decay and insects
UC4A	Ground contact or fresh water (non-critical component)	Permanent wood foundations, building poles, posts, crossties and utility poles (high decay areas)	Decay and insects
UC4B	Ground contact or fresh water (critical component)	Land and fresh water piling, foundation piling, crossties and utility poles (high decay areas)	Decay and insects (high potential)
UC4C	Ground contact or fresh water (critical structural components)	Land and fresh water piling, foundation piling, crossties and utility poles (severe decay areas)	Decay and insects (severe potential)
a. Table is based on AWPA Standard U1			

The treatment level of preserved wood should be matched to the type of service and exposure involved in the application. There are five basic use categories for the specification of treated wood products that relate to increasing levels of exposure. These use categories are described above in Table 10.

In general, most residential applications are found in Use Categories 2 through 4 (UC2 through UC4). An A, B or C following the Use Category further differentiates performance expectations based on risk. (Use Category 5, not shown, applies to salt water-exposure conditions, where significantly greater amounts of treatment are required, such as at pilings, bulkheads, etc.) The Use Category for fire resistance is separately identified as UCFA or UCFB. Because UCFB relates to conditions of exposure to moisture, UCFA-treated lumber and plywood are more common in residential construction where fire resistance may be required by code, such as roof sheathing on townhouses and apartment buildings.

Alternative Foundation Construction Methods

Other types of foundation wall construction methods and materials that are less frequently used in the United States include:

- permanent wood foundations (PWFs);
- insulated concrete forms (ICFs);
- pre-cast concrete foundations; and
- elevated foundations in flood-prone areas.

These systems are not specifically addressed in this book except to mention that there are important foundation moisture-management practices that may be required. The inspector should carefully consider manufacturer and industry-recommended practices, in addition to any relevant minimum building code requirements, when inspecting these other types. With proper consideration and installation, these systems provide dry and serviceable foundation systems.

Moisture Vapor Control

Best Practices for Moisture Vapor Control

This section focuses on best practices to control moisture vapor and the condensation and damp conditions it can cause in a house. The terms "moisture vapor" and "water vapor" are used interchangeably.

General

In the sections covering roofs, the best practices focus on preventing bulk water intrusion through roof, wall and foundation assemblies. Without bulk water intrusion in check, efforts to control moisture vapor may be partially successful at best, and counterproductive at worst. For example, using vapor retarders and sealing air-leakage pathways can be good methods for managing moisture vapor in a wall, but if rainwater is leaking into the wall, then these steps could actually worsen the problem by reducing the wall's ability to dry out. The point here is that practices for managing moisture vapor may also affect bulk water management, and vice-versa, so it's important to consider both issues.

Climate Considerations

In the northern U.S., moisture vapor problems are driven primarily by indoor relative humidity (RH) combined with low outdoor temperatures during the winter. In the southern U.S. (especially the southeast), the problem is largely driven by high outdoor humidity and low indoor temperatures during summer months. Mixed climates are exposed to both conditions and can experience both types of problems. Therefore, many of the best-practice recommendations in this section vary according to climate. The same is true of the underlying building code requirements.

Unfortunately, there is no definitive and widely accepted climate map that addresses all climate factors that contribute to moisture vapor problems. There are perhaps too many variables in climate and construction practices to treat the issue without significant use of experience and judgment. Various climate maps and criteria have been applied in building codes in the past, and more recent building code changes continue to demonstrate a lack of overall agreement among experts. It is for these reasons that accepted practices for moisture vapor control often vary based on local experience and differences of opinion.

This guide attempts to avoid the problem as described above by using three tried-and-true climate maps for the purpose of guiding decisions regarding best practices to address problems associated with moisture vapor intrusion. These maps are shown in Figures 29, 30 and 31. They are not intended to imply any unique degree of certainty in associating climate conditions with appropriate practices for moisture vapor control. They do, however, provide accurate trends in correlating vapor control practices to climate. These should be considered when implementing an appropriate practice locally.

Heating degree days (HDD), as shown on the following page, form the primary basis for defining climate zones used in building codes for energy efficiency and moisture vapor control. For the purpose of discussion of the concepts and best practices in this guide, the following climate regions are approximated based on heating degree days:

- very cold climate: HDD of 8,000 or greater;
- cold climate: HDD of 6,000 to 8,000;
- mixed climate: HDD of 2,500 through 6,000; and
- hot climate: HDD of less than 2,500.

The Decay Hazard Index in Figure 30 reflects the dampness of the climate in terms of the potential for wood decay. It is indirectly related to frequent high outdoor humidity levels. For the purpose of discussion of the concepts and best practices in this guide, the following damp/moisture-related climate zones are approximated based on the Decay Hazard Index:

- damp/humid: Decay Hazard Index of 70 or greater;
- moderately damp: Decay Hazard Index of 35 to 70; and
- dry climate: Decay Hazard Index of less than 35.

Finally, the Condensation Zone Map to follow has been used in the past to help determine which areas that vapor retarders are to be placed on the warm-in-winter side of thermal insulation comprising the thermal envelope of a building. In recent years, either a hot-humid climate criteria or a Heating Degree Day zone may have been used for this purpose. As a result, recommendations for the use of vapor retarders on the warm-in-winter side of above-grade thermal envelopes may vary by as much as several hundred miles to the north or south of the region. The important observation here is the trend of the use of vapor retarders with respect to climate, and that not any one criterion is necessarily a singular directive, except, of course, for local building codes where an inexact directive may become a very specific law.

CANADA
WASHINGTON
MONTANA
NORTH DAKOTA
MINNESOTA
OREGON
IDAHO
SOUTH DAKOTA
WISCONSIN
MICHIGAN
WYOMING
IOWA
NEBRASKA
NEVADA
UTAH
CALIFORNIA
COLORADO
KANSAS
ILLINOIS
INDIANA
OHIO
MISSOURI
KENTUCKY
WEST VIRGINIA
VIRGINIA
OKLAHOMA
TENNESSEE
NORTH CAROLINA
ARIZONA
NEW MEXICO
ARKANSAS
SOUTH CAROLINA
GEORGIA
ALABAMA
MISSISSIPPI
LOUISIANA
TEXAS
FLORIDA
MAINE
NEW YORK
PENNSYLVANIA
VERMONT
NEW HAMPSHIRE
MASSACHUSETTS
RHODE ISLAND
CONNECTICUT
NEW JERSEY
DELAWARE
MARYLAND
DC
PACIFIC OCEAN
ATLANTIC OCEAN
GULF OF MEXICO
MEXICO
THE BAHAMAS
CUBA
Albers equal area projection
0 100 200 300 mi
0 100 200 300 km
The concept of cooling degree days was developed to relate the day's temperature to the energy demands of air conditioning. Cooling degree days are calculated using the day's average temperature minus 65° F.
Annual Cooling Degree Days
less than 101
101–400
401–700
701–1000
1001–1500
1501–2000
2001–2500
2501–3500
more than 3500
Data from the National Environmental Satellite, Data, and Information Service

CANADA
WASHINGTON
MONTANA
NORTH DAKOTA
MINNESOTA
OREGON
IDAHO
SOUTH DAKOTA
WISCONSIN
MICHIGAN
WYOMING
IOWA
NEBRASKA
NEVADA
UTAH
CALIFORNIA
COLORADO
KANSAS
ILLINOIS
INDIANA
OHIO
MISSOURI
KENTUCKY
WEST VIRGINIA
VIRGINIA
OKLAHOMA
TENNESSEE
NORTH CAROLINA
ARIZONA
NEW MEXICO
ARKANSAS
SOUTH CAROLINA
GEORGIA
ALABAMA
MISSISSIPPI
LOUISIANA
TEXAS
FLORIDA
MAINE
NEW YORK
PENNSYLVANIA
VERMONT
NEW HAMPSHIRE
MASSACHUSETTS
RHODE ISLAND
CONNECTICUT
NEW JERSEY
DELAWARE
MARYLAND
DC
PACIFIC OCEAN
ATLANTIC OCEAN
GULF OF MEXICO
MEXICO
THE BAHAMAS
CUBA
Albers equal area projection
0 100 200 300 mi
0 100 200 300 km
The concept of heating degree days was developed to relate the day's temperature to the energy demands of heating fuel. Heating degree days are calculated using the day's average temperature subtracted from 65°F.
Annual Heating Degree Days
less than 1001
1001–2000
2001–3000
3001–4000
4001–5000
5001–6000
6001–7000
7001–9000
more than 9000
Data from the National Environmental Satellite, Data, and Information Service

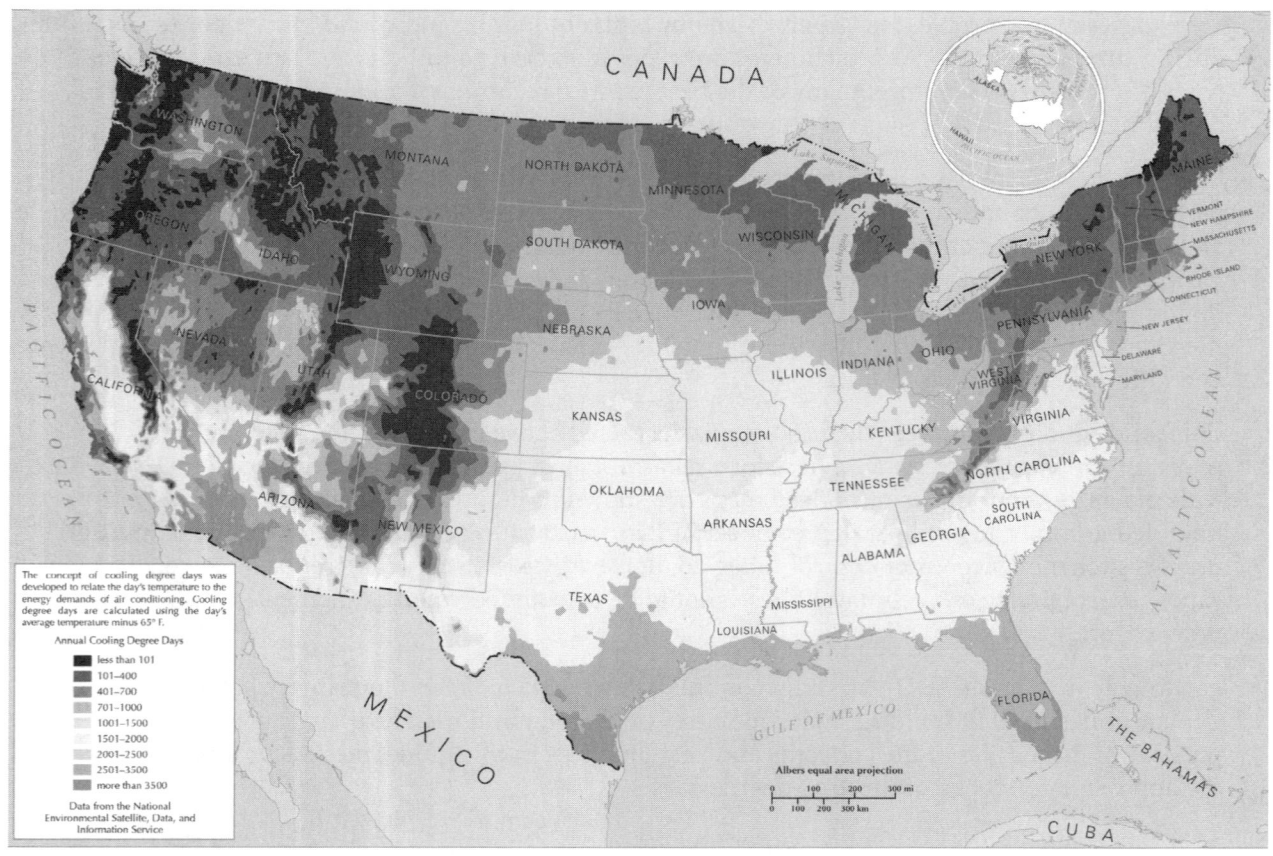

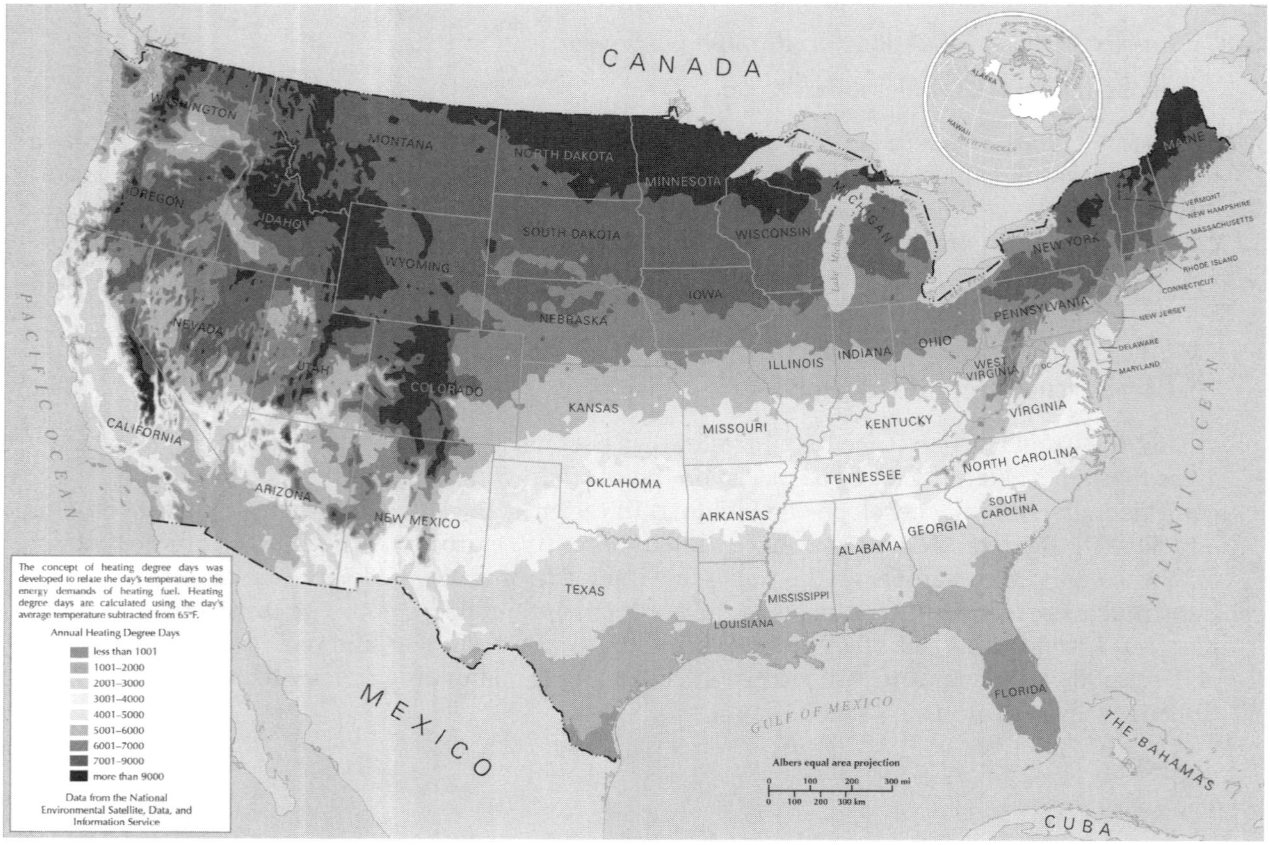

Moisture Vapor Problems

Overview

Moisture problems related to water vapor can be confusing because they're caused by several types of moisture sources and can result from different types of dynamics in a house. Also, seemingly unrelated decisions that are made for one building system, such as how to lay out the HVAC system, are not at all independent and will affect the migration of water vapor in a house.

Water vapor problems typically involve multiple factors, too. Removing one or more of these factors will often correct or prevent a problem from occurring, even in complicated scenarios where several factors are involved. Many water vapor problems can be prevented by addressing a few fundamental issues in houses, such as indoor humidity, air leakage, and the location of the vapor retarder. Addressing these issues with some basic best practices is the focus of the following sections. A selection of more complex design issues related to water vapor control — some of which are controversial issues currently without a clear consensus — are also discussed briefly, with references to other resources.

DECAY HAZARD INDEX

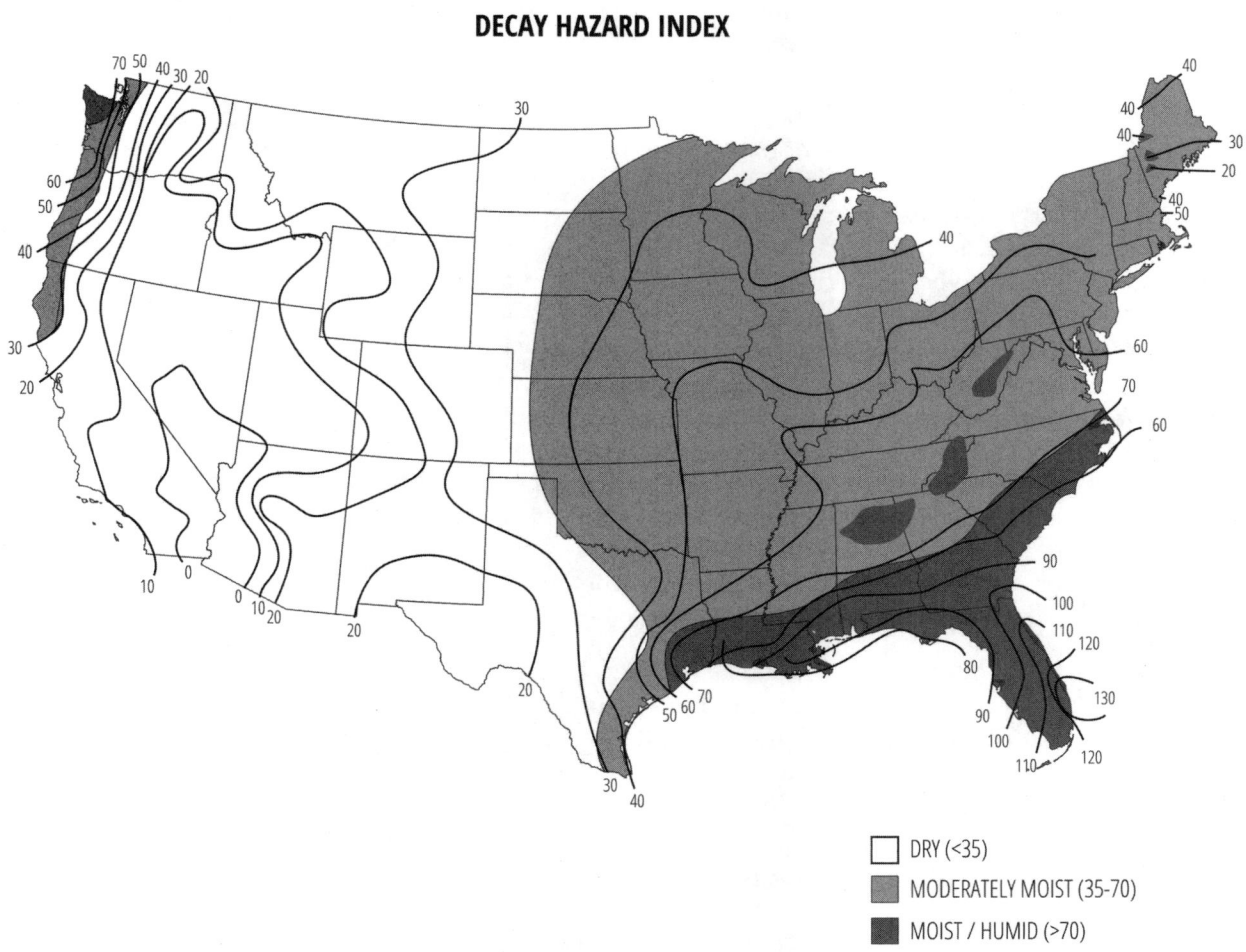

DRY (<35)

MODERATELY MOIST (35-70)

MOIST / HUMID (>70)

Defining the Water Vapor Permeance of Materials

Discussions of water vapor, vapor migration, and vapor retarders require clear definitions. This guide uses a scale of permeance levels common to building codes and other industry literature (as measured in perms, or gr/hr ft² in Hg):

- vapor retarder is < 1 perm;
- vapor impermeability is < 0.1 perms (also called a vapor barrier);
- vapor retarder is semi-impermeable (0.1 to 1 perm);
- vapor retarder is semi-permeable (1 to 10 perms); and
- vapor permeability is > 10 perms.

The permeability or permeance of materials can be measured with ASTM E-96 using the dry-cup method, in which the test sample is evaluated with 0% RH on one side and 50% RH on the other side. It's also important to realize that many materials exhibit different permeance behavior depending on the local humidity levels, which can mean significantly higher perm levels at higher RH. For example, 15-pound asphalt felt has a rating of ~1 perm using the dry-cup method, but 5.6 perms using the wet-cup method, which tests a sample at 50% to 100% RH. Similarly, 1/2-inch OSB varies with humidity, from 0.06 to 1.2 perms (10% to 50% RH) to nearly 4 perms (90% RH). The 2005 ASHRAE Fundamentals Handbook contains permeance data for a range of construction materials. Manufacturers can also provide exact data for specific products.

Indoor Humidity Problems

High indoor humidity (greater than 40% in the winter and greater than 60% in the summer, as a general range) is a primary cause of many vapor-related moisture problems in homes. The following information covers the control of indoor relative humidity (RH) levels in homes. From a moisture perspective, very low indoor relative humidity levels are helpful to control condensation and related problems. But other important factors that actually require some minimum level of indoor RH to be maintained must also be considered. These include a minimum humidity level to keep occupants comfortable (approximately 25%), minimum humidity to keep wood finishes and furniture from drying out, and for homeowners with special needs for higher indoor humidity.

Relative Humidity

When interior RH levels are a concern, whole-house and spot ventilation to the dry, outdoor air could be installed, and ventilation controls that automate spot exhaust could be added. High RH levels might be a concern based on local experience and climate, high expected occupancy loads, unusual occupant habits, or especially tight construction. Providing for increased ventilation means selecting higher-capacity fans for whole-house or local ventilation devices.

One option is continuous fan operation at a low level with local switches that can boost the fan speed temporarily. In humid regions, the addition of damp outdoor air without any treatment of this new moisture load will actually add moisture to the house instead of helping to control indoor RH. Heating, cooling and ventilation systems in such climates should be operated to accommodate additional moisture loads resulting from ventilation.

Document Dehumidification Measures

Inspectors should consider documenting the existence of any supplemental dehumidification that is observed during an inspection. The presence of dehumidifier units may indicate the homeowner's concern about humidity or moisture. Supplemental dehumidification systems address indoor RH by managing both built-in moisture in new houses (like the water that dissipates from a new concrete basement) and ongoing moisture loads in existing homes. Controlling ongoing moisture loads is especially important in areas with humid shoulder seasons, when the A/C system will not operate for cooling but indoor humidity must still be removed. Supplemental dehumidification equipment options are also discussed.

Check for Wet Building Materials

Moisture-sensitive building materials for new construction should be protected from exposure to excessive moisture while being stored on site, and also prior to closing in the building. Wood products, such as structural panels and framing lumber, should be kept under the roof, whenever possible.

If such components cannot be kept under the roof on site, at a minimum, they should be protected and not stored in direct contact with the ground. Components such as wood structural panels should be elevated off the ground on a platform supported by at least three 4x4s (one in the center of the platform, and the other two 12 to 16 inches from each end). The platform should also be covered at the base with a plastic sheet to block the migration of ground moisture up into the stack of panels. Stored panels on the platform should be covered on the top and sides with a plastic sheet that shields the panels from rain snugly enough not to be blown off by winds, but also loosely enough to allow some air circulation around the stack.

In applications where moisture-sensitive materials must be exposed to the weather for a period of time after their installation (before the building is closed in), the homeowner should consider alternative materials that can better withstand moisture. A common example of this is the firewall assembly in townhouse construction, which is often comprised of multiple layers of fired-rated gypsum wallboard between adjacent units. Because these materials are left exposed for some time during construction, alternative materials, such as moisture-resistant gypsum, should be considered in such applications. Drywall manufacturers now produce alternative products for these scenarios and uses.

Building Materials Must Stay Dry

Prior to close-in, building assemblies that may become severely wet during the construction process (such as the exterior walls) should be checked to confirm that they're suitably dry. This is especially important if the wall assembly includes low-permeability materials that will restrict drying of the wall once it's closed in. In addition to avoiding the close-in of wet assemblies that could result in mold or material degradation, checking the moisture content of framing assemblies can also help to protect against excessive wood shrinkage and the damage this causes to interior finishes.

Therefore, a general range of 10% to 15% moisture content (MC) should be confirmed before closing in assemblies and finishing. And to prevent differential shrinkage of materials and finish damage, it's also recommended that wood materials be within about 5% of the wood's equilibrium moisture content (EMC) for the region. So, in areas such as the Southwest, a desert region where equilibrium moisture content is roughly 5% to 6%, lumber at a maximum MC of 10% is preferred before finishing. Using the Decay Hazard Index Map in Figure 30 as a rough indicator of EMC, the following upper limits for lumber moisture before finishing occurs can be used as approximate targets:

- Decay Hazard Index ≤ 20: maximum lumber MC at finish installation = 10%;
- Decay Hazard Index 20 to 70: maximum lumber MC at finish install = 12%; and
- Decay Hazard Index ≥ 70: maximum lumber MC at finish install = 15%.

These regional values are estimates only. You can gain a better feel for the relationship between lumber MC and the durability of finishes by checking moisture levels on every inspection. Moisture meters can be used for this purpose.

Properly Sized Cooling Equipment to Improve Water Vapor Removal

Cooling systems should be properly sized based on the home's construction characteristics and the local climate in order to reduce short-cycling, thereby improving the ability of the system to extract moisture from indoor air. Basic tools for proper cooling system sizing are discussed later in this section.

Educate Homeowners on the Impact of Their Household Habits on RH

Homeowners should be educated on how their habits, such as the use of exhaust fans and humidifiers, can have a major effect on indoor humidity levels.

Air Leakage and Major Moisture Problems

Air leakage through building assemblies can move large quantities of water vapor and is a major factor in many vapor-related moisture problems. Building envelopes should be designed and constructed to reduce air leakage from inside to outside in cold climates, and from outside to inside in hot and humid climates. To achieve this objective, the big leaks in the building's envelope must be sealed. In addition, a suitable air-barrier system should be carefully considered and employed during the construction of the home. Home inspectors should understand air leaks and know where to look for them.

Air leakage is driven by any one or a combination of the following factors: wind; the stack effect; and forced-air HVAC equipment, such as a central air handler. Wind and stack effect-driven air leakage is best handled by the use of air barriers (explained later in this section). HVAC issues are also addressed.

Problems with Sealing Up a House

There are a few precautions worth mentioning for tightening the building envelope. First, the use of air barriers and air-leakage sealing practices can reduce the supply of combustion air for fossil fuel-fired equipment (such as oil and gas furnaces, gas water heaters, gas dryers, etc.) that are located within the conditioned space. This can result in negative pressure and back-drafting of combustion products. The operation of spot exhaust fans (in the kitchen and bath), whole-house exhaust ventilation, or even the stack effect can also cause depressurization of the indoor space near combustion equipment, leading to back-drafting and the introduction of combustion products into the home, such as carbon monoxide. Because of these health and safety concerns, sealed combustion equipment is a good recommendation that is explained later.

Additionally, mechanical ventilation may be required or recommended to address other consequences of tightening the building envelope, such as indoor air quality (IAQ) and humidity control. For example, modern residential building codes still permit the use of operable windows as a means of providing fresh-air ventilation, though this has been hotly contested in recent years. However, it may be increasingly risky to rely solely on occupant behavior to provide adequate ventilation in this manner in the absence of higher levels of natural ventilation.

As a final precaution, air-barrier materials must also be considered in terms of their impact on vapor movement and water shedding. For instance, if an air barrier is used on the exterior of the wall as a weather barrier underneath cladding (housewrap), it must have adequate water-resistant qualities. And if an air barrier is used on the inside of a wall in a hot and humid climate, it needs to be made of a permeable material, and not one that will prevent vapor from drying to the inside.

Look for Big Air Leaks

To ensure that an air barrier functions as intended, leaks in the building envelope and air barrier system must be reasonably controlled. The common-sense methods are generally low-tech. Current building codes require air-sealing around the following types of areas: framing joints around windows, doors and skylights; utility penetrations; drop-ceilings adjacent to the thermal envelope; wall cavities and chases that extend into unconditioned space; walls and ceilings separated from conditioned space by an attached garage; openings behind tub and shower enclosures on exterior walls; common walls between dwelling units; and other sources of air leakage. Sealing materials include acceptable air-barrier materials and durable caulks, sealants, tapes and gaskets, as appropriate.

The above list is exhaustive. All obvious air-leakage pathways are required to be mitigated. Yet, practicality suggests that the major focus should be on the big leaks. Big leakage points that should be air-sealed include: vertical mechanical chases; attic access hatches or pull-down ladders; floor overhangs; openings behind tub and shower enclosures; plumbing stack penetrations; utility penetrations in walls; and any exposed wall cavities that open into an adjacent attic space. Major leakage points commonly found in a house are illustrated in the images that follow. As an inspector, look at these areas.

Sealing the locations mentioned above should involve products that are durable and compatible with the joined materials, especially around hot surfaces. Examples include high-quality caulks, construction adhesives, spray polyurethane foam, gaskets, sill sealers, tapes, and a number of specialty products, such as gasketed electrical receptacles, switch boxes, and ceiling-light fixture boxes.

Check Air Leaks at Cathedral Roofs

Cathedral roofs can hide roof water leaks and condensation, particularly if a vapor retarder, such as polyethylene sheeting, is used on the ceiling side (something that should be considered only in very cold climates). If a cathedral roof is installed, the ceiling and penetrations through the ceiling should be carefully sealed to prevent air leakage. This may involve special air-sealed light fixtures, the use of caulks and sealants at all penetrations and joints, and avoidance of leaky ceiling systems, such as exposed tongue-and-groove boards. Leakage of humid indoor air into cold cathedral roof cavities is a major cause of condensation and moisture problems.

Inspectors Should Know Where an Air Barrier Should Be Installed

Reducing air leakage through the building envelope is a good practice regardless of where in the envelope it takes place. Air-barrier systems are strategies to block air leaks at a certain point in the building assembly while also addressing other envelope concerns, such as rainwater protection and vapor retarders. This section of the book explains basic air-barrier strategies and where to look for them.

Appropriate air-barrier materials include some panel products, membranes, and other coatings that have low air permeability. Examples include gypsum wallboard, spray polyurethane foams, wood structural panels, extruded polystyrene and polyisocyanurate foamboards, building wraps, and other materials. Seams and laps in these products must be sealed.

Examples of products that may be considered too air-permeable to serve as an air barrier include fiberboard, expanded polystyrene insulation (Type I), glass fiber insulation board, and tarred felt paper.

There are basically four methods of providing an air-barrier system. Two of these approaches place the air barrier on the inside of the thermal envelope, and two place the barrier on the exterior.

Why Control Air Leakage?

First, air flow can transfer moisture vapor through and into building assemblies in amounts 10 to 100 times more than that which would typically occur by vapor diffusion. Significant air leaks — from a bathroom into a cold attic, for example — can deposit large amounts of moisture vapor on cool surfaces and create condensation and water accumulation that damage building materials and make some insulation materials ineffective. Without reasonable air-leakage control, the use of vapor barriers is of limited benefit. Similarly, attempts to pressurize a building in a hot and humid climate (to control against the intrusion of outdoor humidity) or depressurize a building in a cold climate are far more effective with a tighter building shell.

Admittedly, some amount of natural air leakage under the right climate conditions can be a good thing. Under ideal conditions that may occur during some periods of the year, it can help to dry building assemblies. Air leakage in the form of intended ventilation in attics and crawlspaces (outside of a building's thermal envelope) is an accepted means of reducing moisture and is effective in many climates. Air leakage through the thermal envelope can also allow for uncontrolled natural ventilation of the building for indoor air quality.

However, the benefits of air infiltration through a building's thermal envelope are either undependable or risky in many climates. Therefore, dependence on excessive or uncontrolled air leakage through modern building thermal envelope systems is generally discouraged. And, in fact, modern model building and energy codes usually require fairly extensive practices to prevent the uncontrolled leakage of air through a building's thermal envelope.

Interior Air-Barrier Methods:

- airtight drywall approach (ADA); and
- airtight polyethylene approach (APA).

Exterior Air-Barrier Methods:

- airtight sheathing approach (ASA); and
- airtight wrap approach (AWA).

In cold and very cold climates, the primary concern is preventing interior warm and humid air from flowing outward into a building's exterior envelope assemblies during winter months. This air flow can carry a large amount of moisture and cause condensation in the wall. Therefore, the use of an interior air-barrier system in cold and very cold climates is preferred and may be combined with a warm-in-winter vapor retarder. A viable approach in such regions is the ADA method used in conjunction with an interior vapor-retarder layer, such as kraft-faced batts or vapor-barrier paint on drywall. Use of the APA method should be applied more cautiously, as some localities and building scientists are concerned that the poly layer is almost too airtight and vapor-impermeable, and so will not allow drying to the interior of the building at any time of year.

In damp and humid climates, the primary concern is preventing exterior warm and humid air from leaking inward through exterior surfaces into building envelope assemblies that will be cool from air-conditioning. In damp and humid climates, an air-barrier system is preferred on the outside of the wall. Many exterior sheathing products and wraps can provide this function, and can also serve the water-barrier function underneath siding materials (the ASA and AWA methods).

In climates with mixed conditions, the most suitable air-barrier system can be selected based on other construction characteristics, and then combined with these systems. For example, if building wrap is used as part of a drained-cavity, weather-resistant envelope, then the airtight wrap approach (AWA) can be used with a little extra detailing of the building wrap, such as taping the overlapped seams. Similarly, extra attention to sealing interior drywall joints and penetrations can make the airtight drywall approach (ADA) a reasonable strategy.

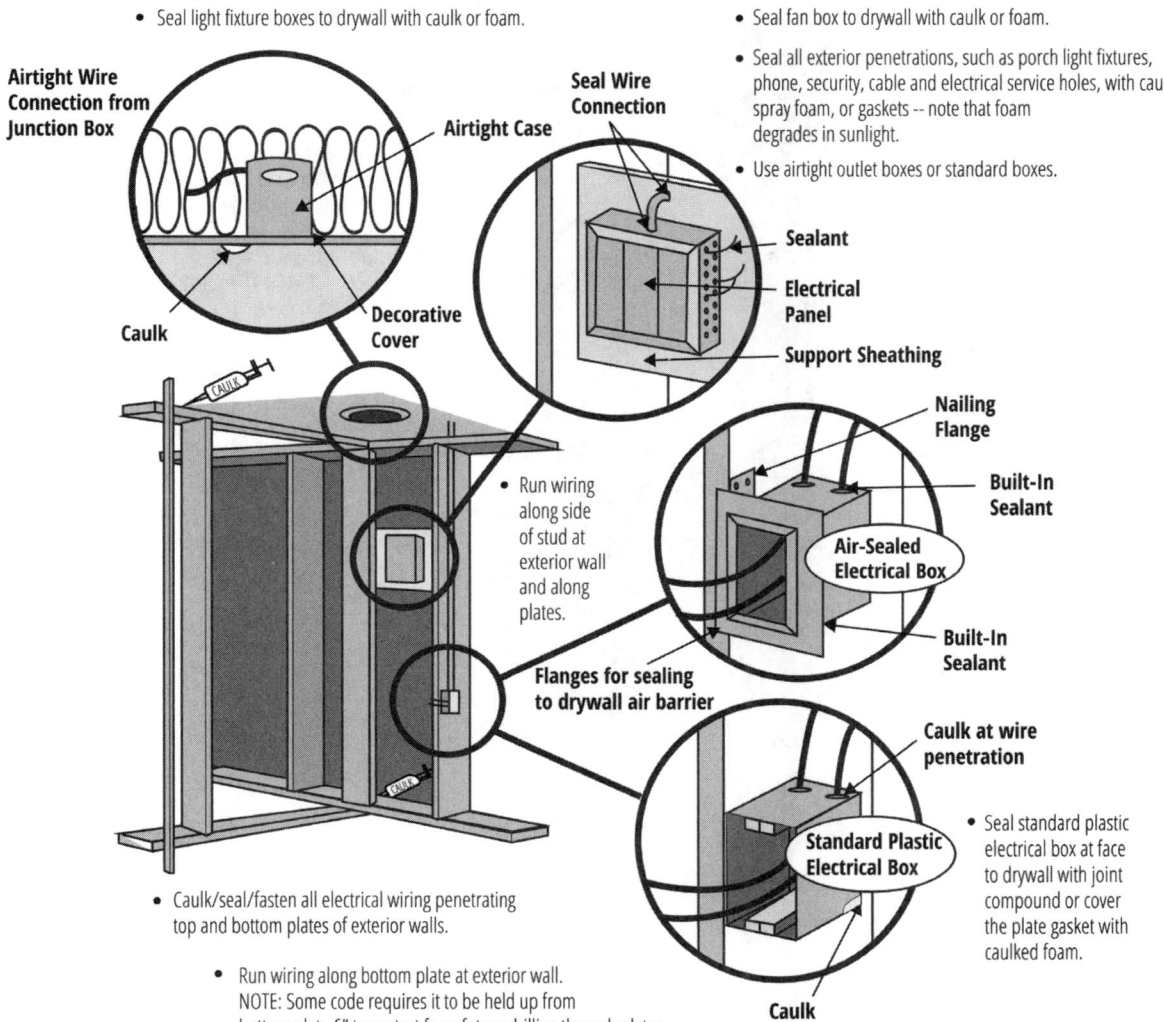

- Recessed light fixtures should be rated for Insulated Ceiling Air Tight (ICAT).
- Ceiling fans should be wired to a wall switch.
- Seal light fixture boxes to drywall with caulk or foam.
- Seal fan box to drywall with caulk or foam.
- Seal all exterior penetrations, such as porch light fixtures, phone, security, cable and electrical service holes, with caulk, spray foam, or gaskets -- note that foam degrades in sunlight.
- Use airtight outlet boxes or standard boxes.

Airtight Wire Connection from Junction Box

Seal Wire Connection

Airtight Case

Caulk

Decorative Cover

Sealant

Electrical Panel

Support Sheathing

Nailing Flange

Built-In Sealant

Air-Sealed Electrical Box

Built-In Sealant

- Run wiring along side of stud at exterior wall and along plates.

Flanges for sealing to drywall air barrier

Caulk at wire penetration

Standard Plastic Electrical Box

- Seal standard plastic electrical box at face to drywall with joint compound or cover the plate gasket with caulked foam.

Caulk

- Caulk/seal/fasten all electrical wiring penetrating top and bottom plates of exterior walls.

- Run wiring along bottom plate at exterior wall. NOTE: Some code requires it to be held up from bottom plate 6" to protect from future drilling through plates.

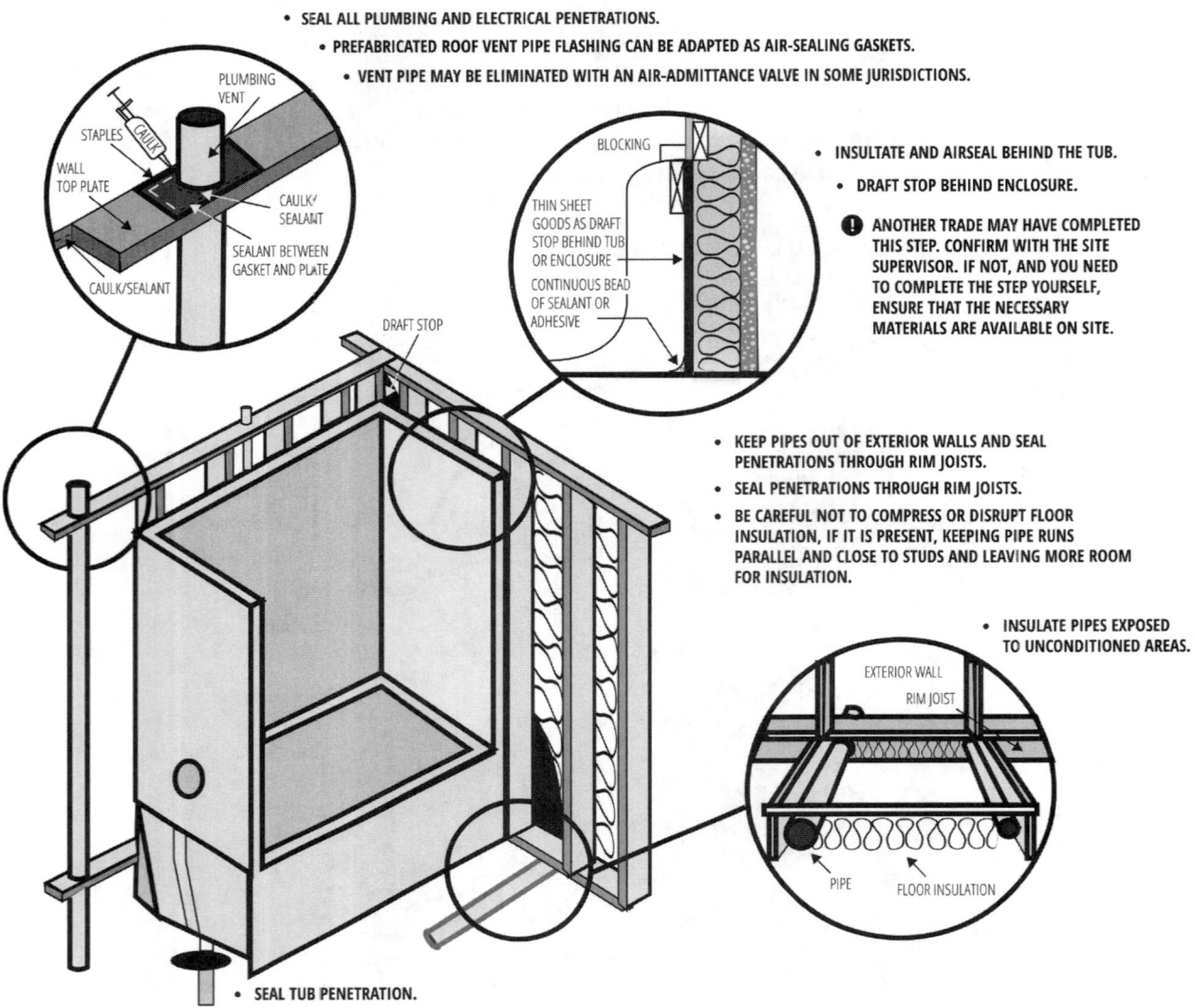

- SEAL ALL PLUMBING AND ELECTRICAL PENETRATIONS.
  - PREFABRICATED ROOF VENT PIPE FLASHING CAN BE ADAPTED AS AIR-SEALING GASKETS.
  - VENT PIPE MAY BE ELIMINATED WITH AN AIR-ADMITTANCE VALVE IN SOME JURISDICTIONS.

PLUMBING VENT
STAPLES
CAULK
WALL TOP PLATE
CAULK/ SEALANT
SEALANT BETWEEN GASKET AND PLATE
CAULK/SEALANT

BLOCKING
THIN SHEET GOODS AS DRAFT STOP BEHIND TUB OR ENCLOSURE
CONTINUOUS BEAD OF SEALANT OR ADHESIVE

- INSULTATE AND AIRSEAL BEHIND THE TUB.
- DRAFT STOP BEHIND ENCLOSURE.
- ANOTHER TRADE MAY HAVE COMPLETED THIS STEP. CONFIRM WITH THE SITE SUPERVISOR. IF NOT, AND YOU NEED TO COMPLETE THE STEP YOURSELF, ENSURE THAT THE NECESSARY MATERIALS ARE AVAILABLE ON SITE.

DRAFT STOP

- KEEP PIPES OUT OF EXTERIOR WALLS AND SEAL PENETRATIONS THROUGH RIM JOISTS.
- SEAL PENETRATIONS THROUGH RIM JOISTS.
- BE CAREFUL NOT TO COMPRESS OR DISRUPT FLOOR INSULATION, IF IT IS PRESENT, KEEPING PIPE RUNS PARALLEL AND CLOSE TO STUDS AND LEAVING MORE ROOM FOR INSULATION.

- INSULATE PIPES EXPOSED TO UNCONDITIONED AREAS.

EXTERIOR WALL
RIM JOIST
PIPE   FLOOR INSULATION

- SEAL TUB PENETRATION.

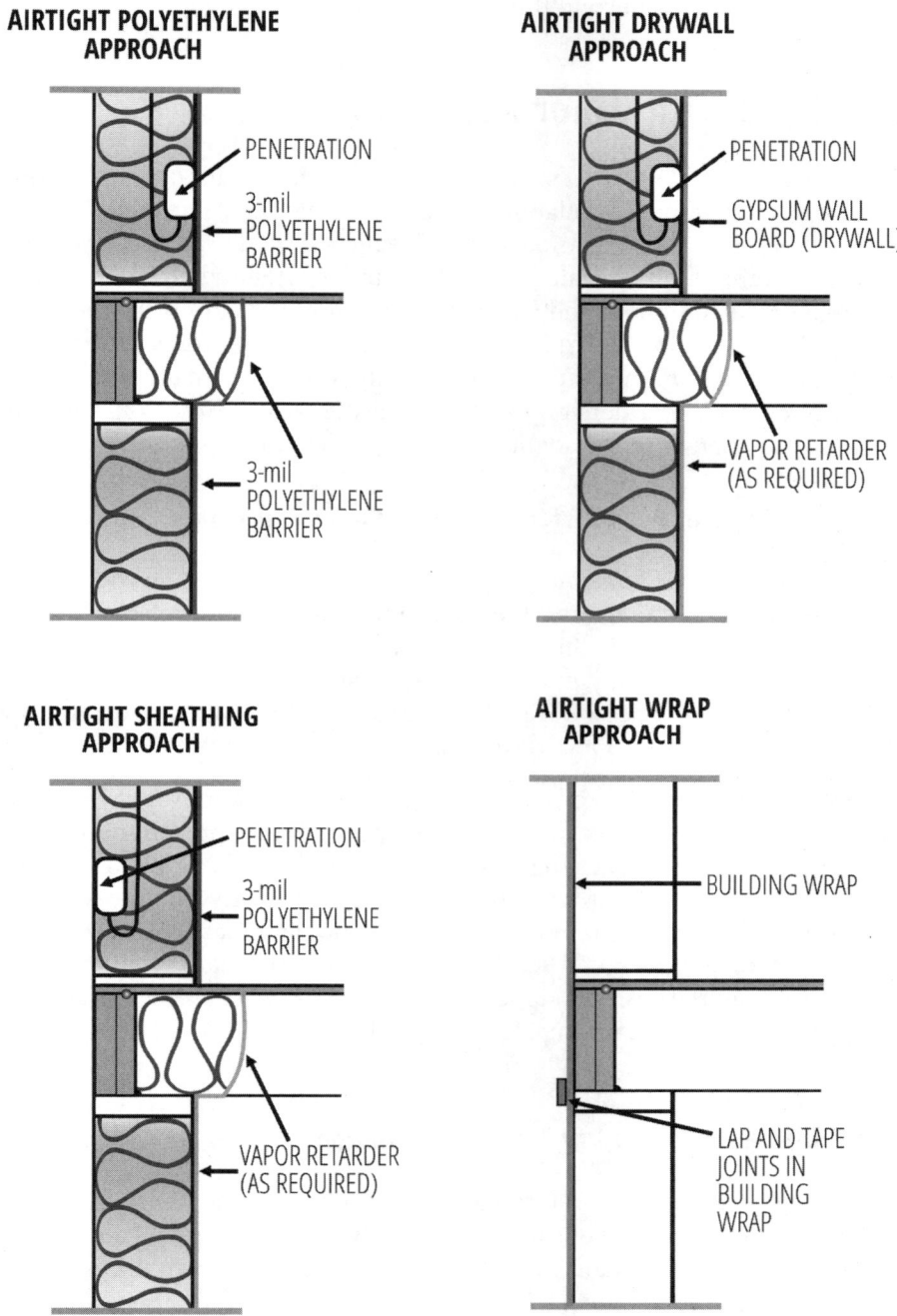

AIRTIGHT POLYETHYLENE
APPROACH

PENETRATION

3-mil
POLYETHYLENE
BARRIER

3-mil
POLYETHYLENE
BARRIER

AIRTIGHT DRYWALL
APPROACH

PENETRATION

GYPSUM WALL
BOARD (DRYWALL)

VAPOR RETARDER
(AS REQUIRED)

AIRTIGHT SHEATHING
APPROACH

PENETRATION

3-mil
POLYETHYLENE
BARRIER

VAPOR RETARDER
(AS REQUIRED)

AIRTIGHT WRAP
APPROACH

BUILDING WRAP

LAP AND TAPE
JOINTS IN
BUILDING
WRAP

Blower Doors: Useful Tool for Gauging Air-Leakage Control Practices

A blower door test to evaluate the effectiveness of air-leakage control strategy is useful for models that will be repetitively built or for quality control purposes on any home. Blower door testing can be conducted on a finished house, or alternatively on a house that is insulated, sealed, but with walls not yet closed in. Testing at a pre-completion stage of construction will not provide a useful numerical result, but it can be very helpful for clearly observing where leakage in the envelope is occurring through the use of a smoke pencil device that indicates drafts. Blower door tests on a finished house may also be used to determine whether supplemental ventilation may be necessary for indoor air quality purposes.

The use of a blower door goes beyond the scope of a home inspection.

Major Problems with Vapor Retarders

Many moisture-related problems and structural damage that are discovered by home inspectors can be traced back to improper installation of the vapor retarders. The component is often simply installed in the wrong location. The movement of water vapor via vapor diffusion is a major factor of water vapor problems in houses, along with high indoor RH and air leakage. The objective of this section is for inspectors to understand best-practice recommendations for the correct use of vapor retarders in the above-grade portion of a building's thermal envelope. Knowing what a properly installed barrier looks like will help an inspector easily recognize a barrier that is improperly installed. The use of vapor retarders on foundation systems is addressed in the following sections, and covers the unique nature of foundation moisture exposure.

Making the Right Choice: Air Barrier Approaches and Materials

The selection of an air-barrier strategy and material should not be made without also considering the exterior weather-barrier system and the appropriate use of vapor retarding materials. The best choices will achive all goals for the building envelope — e.g., weather-resistant barrier, appropriate inner and outer vapor permeability, energy efficiency, structural performance, fire resistance, etc. — as well as cost-effectiveness. Because of the variety of considerations, many viable solutions are possible with consideration of local building codes and local material preferences.

Vapor retarders are used to control or slow the diffusion of moisture vapor through building envelope materials. Vapor retarders, when applied appropriately, prevent high levels of humidity inside building envelope assemblies that can result in condensation. When applied or installed incorrectly, vapor retarders can trap moisture, slow the normal drying process, and contribute to moisture damage. As mentioned in the previous section, air leakage is a more dominant type of water vapor movement, but vapor retarders also play an important role in an overall moisture-control strategy. All materials exhibit some amount of vapor retardance; that is, they have some impact on allowing moisture vapor to pass through them. Inspectors should understand that all materials play some role in water vapor migration.

In Hot-Humid Climates, Walls Dry Toward the Inside

In hot-humid climates, exterior wall systems should dry toward the interior by locating vapor-retarding materials on the outside of the wall assembly, and keeping interior materials vapor-permeable. Providing some resistance to outdoor moisture vapor from diffusing into the wall assembly limits moisture problems during hot and humid periods of the year. And by keeping the interior side of the assembly vapor-permeable, any moisture within the wall system can migrate to the cool and dry building interior.

If a vapor-retarding material, such as polyethylene or vinyl wallpaper, is installed toward the inside of the wall assembly, it could block vapor migration on its cool surface and cause condensation problems. Instead, materials installed toward the interior of the wall assembly should be semi-permeable or permeable, such as unfaced fiberglass batts with permeable interior paint on the gypsum. And while any practices related to vapor retarders and other wall-assembly materials are subject to local code requirements, the damp and humid areas described earlier give an indication of where drying to the interior is most important.

Inspecting "Warm Walls" in Cold Climates

For cold climates, some current building science research recommends avoiding the use of sheathing materials that are low-perm and also of little insulating value (e.g., wood structural panels and similar sheathing) in climates with a substantial winter season. The concern is that the inside face of these materials will create a cold surface during cold weather, and if humid indoor air enters the wall from air leakage or vapor diffusion, it will condense on this surface. Condensation that does form in this manner would be unable to dry outwards through the sheathing, since the sheathing is low-perm.

Furthermore, when an exterior insulating sheathing is used that also happens to be a low-perm material, the available research and experience on such wall systems suggests that it should have enough R-value to keep its inside face from reaching a cold enough temperature to cause condensation for any significant period of time. This type of design may be called a "warm wall" approach. For this concept to work without creating a cold condensation surface internal to the wall, the exterior insulating sheathing must be thick enough to minimize the potential for its inside face to reach the dew-point temperature, given a reasonable winter design condition (e.g., indoor and outdoor temperature and humidity). Current building codes do not explicitly address this design approach to moisture vapor control in walls. Building energy codes generally recommend an R-value for insulating sheathing of approximately one-third of the required overall wall insulation R-value, including cavity insulation.

While this book acknowledges current research in these areas, documentation of these issues and well-established best practices are lacking standardized design and construction rules. Regardless, this method is frequently used with success in colder climates because of the condensation control provided by a properly executed "warm wall" design approach.

In hot-humid regions, walls must be able to dry to the inside. Homeowners in hot-humid regions must be educated to not limit the ability of the walls to dry toward the interior by adding non-breathable interior finishes on exterior walls. Finishes that could compromise the wall's ability to dry inward include vinyl wallpaper and vapor-barrier paints.

In Cold Climates, Walls Dry Toward the Outside

In cold climates, exterior wall systems should dry toward the outside by locating vapor-retarding materials on the inside of the wall assembly, and making sure that exterior materials are vapor-permeable. Along with that, control of indoor humidity levels and air leakage are also very important issues. To establish resistance to moisture vapor diffusing into the wall from inside the house, widely accepted materials include kraft-faced insulation batts and semi-permeable interior paints. And while practices related to vapor retarders and other wall assembly materials are subject to local code requirements, the regions north of the condensation line in the climate maps presented earlier indicate areas where the ability to dry toward the exterior is important. As the climate becomes cold (> 6,000 HDD), this issue becomes even more critical because longer and colder winter conditions require walls that can dry outward and assemblies that can limit indoor moisture from entering the wall.

Along with using vapor-retarder materials (such as kraft-faced batts) toward the inside of cold-region wall assemblies, vapor-permeable materials installed toward the outside of the assembly will facilitate outward drying. This allows any moisture in the wall to dry outward toward the colder and drier outdoor environment. However, several common sheathing materials, such as wood structural panels and foam insulating panels, have fairly low perm ratings, which, in theory, could impede drying, and possibly even create a cold surface for condensation. These issues are still being researched by the building science community.

Mechanical Systems and Moisture Control

This section describes moisture-control and moisture-related problems concerning the design, installation and operation of mechanical systems, such as heating and cooling equipment, ductwork and ventilation. Common moisture issues that can arise from residential mechanical systems are covered. No single building system acts in isolation, and seemingly unrelated building systems can actually impact each other in very significant ways. Nowhere is it more relevant than when considering how the mechanical systems might impact the moisture performance of a house. And because some of these inter-relationships are not necessarily obvious, it is important for an inspector to study moisture-related problems in relation to mechanical systems.

Cooling Equipment May Not Be Sized Properly

Dating back at least to the 1958 edition of the FHA's Minimum Property Standards, residential building and energy codes have required that heating and cooling equipment sizes be based upon a recognized calculation method. Modern building and energy codes continue to adhere to this requirement, and an ACCA Manual J analysis is considered the industry standard. Residential cooling systems should, therefore, be sized based upon a house-specific load calculation using Manual J or a comparable analysis and sizing tool. The specific orientation of the house should also be accounted for in this analysis because a change in direction can result in a significantly different design load and equipment size.

A Rule of Thumb for Inspectors

Commonplace rule-of-thumb sizing methods (such as "1 ton of cooling per 400 ft² of conditioned floor area") should not be used in place of a building-specific load calculation method (e.g., Manual J) for reasons described in the text. However, if a rule of thumb has any useful application, it is limited to providing a quick means to determine, during a home inspection, if a particular A/C system design is potentially oversized. In this very limited application, a rule of thumb for hot-humid climates resulting from a 1999 FSEC research study is: cooling capacity = 1/2 ton + 1 ton per 800 ft² of floor area served. Used as a screening tool, rules of thumb that reflect the regional climate and building practices can potentially help home inspectors check mechanical systems for over-sizing.

Intentional over-sizing of A/C systems (or over-sizing, which results from rule-of-thumb methods) causes increased short-cycling of the cooling equipment. Short-cycling reduces energy efficiency and can decrease the moisture-vapor (latent-heat) removal capability of conventional A/C equipment by as much as one-half of the rated latent-heat removal capacity. This has two negative effects. First, indoor relative humidity levels are increased as the A/C system reduces the air temperature but removes moisture to a much lesser extent. Second, due to increased indoor humidity and discomfort, occupants may lower the thermostat set-point temperature to compensate. As a result of cooler indoor temperatures (approximately less than 75° F) and higher indoor RH levels, condensation is more likely to occur on windows and doors, on the inside of wall cavities, on concrete floor surfaces, and on floor sheathing and joists above crawlspaces.

For these reasons, this guide emphasizes the importance of using ACCA Manual J or other similar cooling-load calculation procedures to size HVAC equipment.

Variable-Speed Blowers Improve Moisture Removal

Even with proper sizing of heat pumps for heating and cooling loads, there are significant times of the season when systems will operate under part-load conditions rather than design-load conditions. Thus, accurate sizing of equipment only lessens the short-cycling problem. To provide improved moisture removal and energy efficiency, two-speed compressor heat pumps with variable-speed blowers should be considered. These systems operate on the lower capacity much of the time, providing enhanced moisture removal and more efficient operation. Such systems offer the greatest benefits in areas with long cooling seasons, and are also a good match for two-zone systems because they can effectively handle single- or dual-zone operation.

Supplemental Dehumidification Controlling Indoor Humidity in Damp-Humid Regions

Supplemental dehumidification — or enhanced moisture removal from HVAC equipment — is recommended in damp-humid regions as a means to control indoor moisture levels. In other areas with less prolonged periods of high humidity, these systems should still be considered based on their benefits, such as better control of indoor moisture, enhanced comfort, and integration with fresh-air ventilation.

For new basement foundations, supplemental dehumidification will also help remove moisture from the foundation as it dries, which can help prevent moisture problems in finished basements.

"Supplemental" means some type of dehumidification equipment besides the house A/C system. These systems range in cost, quality and function. A few dehumidification system options are discussed as follows:

- portable dehumidifiers: These are the simplest of supplemental dehumidifiers and generally provide adequate dehumidification for a small volume of air (one room or a small basement). They are relatively inexpensive and can include humidity sensors and controls that regulate their operation. These units may require frequent attention to ensure that they are disposing of condensate properly (unless they are plumbed to a drain). They also give off waste heat into the area where they're located. When a portable dehumidifier is observed during a home inspection, its existence and operation should be documented. It may be an indication of a moisture-related concern or problem being addressed by the property owners or occupants.

- stationary dehumidifiers: These systems are available in a range of sizes for small and large jobs. Their designs include stand-alone, single-zone systems, or they may be incorporated into a forced-air duct system. These systems, which also give off waste heat, have the advantage of a plumbed condensate drain that does not require frequent attention.

- dehumidifier ventilators: These systems are also stand-alone systems used to dehumidify air, but they also include capabilities for fresh-air ventilation and air filtering. Their ability to introduce and dehumidify outdoor air with a single unit mitigates the moisture that ventilation air can bring into a house, which is a major concern in hot-humid climates. Furthermore, since dehumidifying ventilators are an independent piece of equipment, they can be used to control indoor humidity during shoulder seasons when the central A/C system does not run — another big issue in hot-humid climates.

Sealed Combustion Chambers Should Not Create Moisture Problems

The use of sealed-combustion HVAC equipment is ideal because it helps to alleviate potential back-drafting, and it also helps to control pressure differences across the building envelope. Controlling air-pressure differences across the building envelope helps to minimize air leakage and the migration of moisture into building assemblies. Sealed combustion equipment, such as a sealed-combustion natural gas furnace, draws all air for combustion directly from outdoors via a dedicated duct, and combusts the air and fuel in a sealed combustion chamber.

Sealed Ducts Reduce Air Leakage and Moisture

Building codes require that joints in duct systems be made "substantially" airtight by means of tapes, mastics, gaskets, or other approved methods. This guide recommends sealing duct systems such that air leakage to the outside of the building envelope is ≤ 5.0 cfm 25/100 ft² of floor area served by the system.

The measurement "cfm 25" denotes the air leakage from the duct system measured at a duct pressure of 25 pascals. Actual testing of duct systems with a duct-blaster test can be conducted by home energy raters or utilities. Suitable sealing materials include UL 181-rated foil tape and mastic.

Sealing air leakage from ducts has two important advantages. First, it improves HVAC system energy efficiency and, second, it reduces pressure imbalances that can cause air leakage through the building envelope. This air leakage can transfer a large amount of moisture into building assemblies and cause condensation and related problems. For example, a house with leaky supply ducts in the attic can become depressurized, resulting in warm, damp outdoor air being drawn into the building envelope during the cooling season, a particularly troublesome problem in hot-humid climates.

Conversely, building pressurization from leaky return ducts can cause humid indoor air to exfiltrate into the thermal envelope where it may condense on cold surfaces during winter conditions.

Inadequate Air Returns Cause Moisture Problems

Most central return systems do not provide adequate pathways when interior doors are closed because door undercuts do not provide enough flow area for the return air. As a result, some interior spaces become pressurized and others become depressurized. Both of these conditions can drive air leakage and moisture transfer.

An ideal return-air system provides unrestricted pathways for return air to travel to return grilles. To achieve this type of return system, the inspector should see:

- multiple returns, with the ducts formed from actual duct materials, and not building cavities, such as joist bays (the most expensive alternative, but also the most effective); or
- jumper ducts and transfer grilles to provide return-air passageways from rooms that can be isolated when interior doors are closed (which is moderately effective and moderately expensive, but may carry privacy objections).

What's That Dark Stain at the Carpeting's Perimeter?

In addition to alleviating pressure imbalances and limiting air leakage through the building envelope, these practices can also improve comfort and eliminate soiling problems that leave darkened stains on the perimeter of carpets.

Air-Distribution System Commissioning

Building codes require and experts recommend that air-distribution systems (ductwork) be designed in accordance with accepted calculation methodologies (e.g., ACCA Manual D), but as-built systems can often end up remarkably different from the planned design. This is true for both central heating and cooling systems as well as mechanical ventilation equipment. For this reason, many experts also recommend commissioning air-distribution systems in new residences. The process is fairly simple but does require some specialized equipment and time. A typical air-distribution system commissioning process in a house involves the following steps:

- running the HVAC (or ventilation) system once the house is substantially complete;
- measuring flows at supply outlets and return grilles using a flow hood. If individual supply lines have dampers, flow levels can be adjusted to match the design;
- checking the pressure differentials between the central return zone and rooms with doors closed using a pressure gauge. A typical "acceptable" pressure difference between these zones is 5 pascals; and
- checking for correct operation of system controls, such as thermostats, humidistats, dampers and timers (in the case of ventilation equipment).

The findings from these steps can be used to identify any performance issues and ensure that a system that costs thousands of dollars to purchase and install actually performs as intended.

Whole-House Mechanical Ventilation Is Good

Whole-house mechanical ventilation systems are recommended to provide fresh air and help control a range of indoor air contaminants. Systems should be designed based on the ASHRAE Standard 62.2: "Ventilation and Acceptable Indoor Air Quality in Low-Rise Residential Buildings." The benefits of having a whole-house ventilation fan installed can be conveyed to the homeowner-client.

A wide range of potential ventilation systems may be used, from high-end equipment that introduces, filters and dehumidifies outdoor air based on flexible controls, all the way to basic, low-cost systems that simply run a duct from the outdoors into the return-air plenum. Beyond sizing systems appropriately, a number of other design issues should be considered:

- For cold climates, consider ventilation systems that are balanced (air out = air in), or exhaust-based. By keeping the indoor environment at a neutral or slightly negative pressure relative to the outdoors, moist indoor air is not forced outward into cold building assemblies, where it can condense. However, it is critical that exhaust systems do not create negative pressure levels great enough to cause back-drafting or other combustion-appliance safety concerns.
- Ventilation systems in cold climates may also include systems with heat recovery. For example, a heat-recovery ventilator (HRV) exchanges heat from incoming cold air with exhausting conditioned air for reasonably energy-efficient ventilation. The incoming dry air also serves to control indoor humidity levels. Because an HRV matches the incoming and outgoing air flows, this type of system provides balanced ventilation.
- For damp-humid climates, consider supply ventilation systems that pressurize the indoor environment. They help prevent the infiltration of hot and humid outdoor air into building assemblies, where it can condense.
- Another important feature of whole-house ventilation systems for hot and humid climates is accounting for the added moisture load introduced into the house. In such areas, the additional latent moisture load should be addressed either through direct dehumidification in the ventilation system, or through the use of supplemental dehumidification.
- Finally, testing and balancing of mechanical ventilation systems is also recommended, especially when contractors are installing whole-house ventilation. Simple devices, such as flow gauges, can help to ensure that systems operate close to their design-flow rates. In many cases, as-built installations achieve only half of the intended air flow, and controls and timers may not be installed correctly. Building diagnostics firms and home energy raters can often provide this type of service.

Check That All Exhaust Ducts Terminate Outside

It is not uncommon for a home inspector to find clothes dryers vented to an indoor or enclosed building space, such as the crawlspace. It is also common to find bathroom exhaust fans vented to an attic space, or merely directed toward an attic vent. These practices are prone to create moisture vapor problems and should be avoided. Home inspectors should recommend that all exhaust vents be directly vented to the outside by attachment of exhaust-vent ducting to appropriate through-wall or through-roof ventilation fixtures or grilles. Exhaust ventilation ducts should also be attached and supported like any other ductwork. Finally, exhaust fans are rated (e.g., 50 cfm) based on a limited amount of back-pressure due to the type and length of ductwork and bends in the ductwork. Therefore, duct lengths longer than 25 feet (less 5 feet for each 90-degree bend) should be avoided unless appropriately designed. If long duct runs are unavoidable, larger-capacity fan units could be used.

Quiz #4

1. Decay of common wood framing materials can begin when the moisture content of untreated wood exceeds ___%.

    ☐ 5
    ☐ 20
    ☐ 30
    ☐ 100

2. One of the oldest and most trustworthy practices used to prevent wood and other moisture-sensitive materials from decaying is _____ a constant uptake of moisture from the ground.

    ☐ separation from
    ☐ contact with
    ☐ inadequate clearance from
    ☐ direct connection with

3. T/F: The use of CCA (chromated copper arsenate) has been discontinued as a wood treatment except in certain commercial and agricultural applications.

    ☐ True
    ☐ False

4. T/F: A vapor retarder is defined as having < 1 perm based on a scale of permeance levels common to building codes and other industry literature.

    ☐ True
    ☐ False

5. T/F: High indoor humidity is a primary cause of many vapor-related moisture problems in homes.

    ☐ True
    ☐ False

6. T/F: On a home construction site, it is acceptable for wood products to be stored in direct contact with the ground.

    ☐ True
    ☐ False

7. _____ leakage through building assemblies can move large quantities of water vapor and is a major factor in many vapor-related moisture problems.

    ☐ Air

    ☐ Gaseous

    ☐ Sewer

    ☐ Gravitational

8. T/F: Leakage of humid indoor air into cold cathedral roof cavities is a major cause of condensation and moisture problems.

    ☐ True

    ☐ False

9. T/F: Air flow can transfer moisture vapor through and into building assemblies in amounts 10 to 100 times more than that which would typically occur by vapor diffusion.

    ☐ True

    ☐ False

10. When installed incorrectly, vapor retarders can trap _____, slow the normal drying process, and contribute to _____ damage.

    ☐ air..... significant

    ☐ gases..... water

    ☐ moisture..... moisture

    ☐ droplet..... air

11. T/F: In cold climates, exterior wall systems should dry toward the outside by locating vapor-retarding materials on the inside of the wall assembly, and making sure that exterior materials are vapor-permeable.

    ☐ True

    ☐ False

Answer Key is on page 117.

Part 3: Construction-Phase Inspections

This section of the guide offers tips on inspecting for many of the construction and building practices covered in Part 2. When properly installed or implemented during construction, those construction components will aid in making a house moisture-resistant. Property inspectors who perform construction-phase inspections have a unique opportunity to inspect for these building practices and recommend that they be implemented.

Even with a well-designed house and building, plans that call out important details to manage water (the goals of Part 2), job site quality-management and periodic inspections are critical.

Inspectors are often hired to oversee each phase of the construction of a home. Just a few minutes of oversight or inspection at the right point in the construction process can be the difference between applying a best practice or missing that opportunity. And, in many cases, once the opportunity to apply a best practice has passed, it's very difficult and costly to address the issue later on. Considering these simple quality-management measures can help tremendously in avoiding job site moisture problems.

Many of the recommendations in Table 12 to follow are cross-referenced to the construction practices described in Part 2 for further background on a particular item. And, as is the case throughout this entire book, these recommendations are general guidelines that may be used in addition to the knowledge of the inspector that is based on local experience and judgment.

OverSeeIt.com

List yourself in **OverSeeIt.com**. OverSeeIt.com helps consumers who are having a home built, remodeled or repaired find a certified inspector who can make sure the work is being performed properly. OverSeeIt inspectors offer a variety of services, such as project and contractor oversight, new construction-phase inspections, final walk-through inspections, one-year builder warranty inspections, annual inspections for home and commercial property owners, investor consulting, pre-listing and seller inspections, foreclosure inspections, insurance inspections, and general home inspections. There is no cost to be listed. Visit **www.OverSeeIt.com**

Construction-Phase Inspections

Table 12, which appears on the following two pages, delineates the components, aspects and phases of construction that are covered in Part 2 of this handbook. The table can be used to understand the specific installations and points during new-home construction so that you can inspect and document these details in your home inspection report.

Table 12: Construction-Phase Inspection	
Phase of Construction	Building plans should have clear details for controlling moisture. Moisture-control details should be called out in building plans and be easily readable and understood.
Contractors	Contractors should clearly understand material specs and details that are consistent with the building plans. Contractors should be able to address tasks that can be overlooked or dismissed between different subcontractors, such as insulating under a bay window, or air-sealing trunk duct penetrations.
Foundation	Ensure that critical slab features are in place prior to pouring. Prior to slabs being poured, check that poly, gravel beds, insulation and reinforcement are installed as specified. Poly should be directly beneath the slab and be continuous and without tears.
Framing	Check treated lumber's certificates and labels. When preservative-treated wood is used, check that lumber with the specified level of treatment has been delivered.
Framing	Protection of moisture-sensitive materials: check for proper storage of framing materials already on site, and check for proper storage practices as soon as new materials arrive on site.
Framing and Weather-Barrier Installation	Check key features of the weather-resistant envelope before siding is installed. The key features of the building envelope designed to hold moisture out (such as shingle-style, lapped seams on housewrap, and the integration of a weather barrier with flashing details at windows and doors) need to be checked before siding is applied and covers up these details.
Window and Door Installation	Inspect window and door installation procedures. Because penetrations in the building envelope are a common cause of water problems, inspections of window and door installations are needed. Ensure that the flashing is installed properly.
Window Installation	Verify window ratings from product labels and certifications. Window ratings for wind pressure and impact-resistance (if applicable) could be checked on site.
Prior to Foundation Backfill	Inspect the foundation walls for waterproofing and unsealed penetrations. Prior to backfill, the foundation walls should be inspected for waterproofing to specifications, and for penetrations due to voids or other problem areas (such as form ties). Voids in the waterproofing should be appropriately repaired and sealed to create a waterproof face.

Table 12: Construction-Phase Inspection	
Prior to Backfill	Inspect backfill and grading for compliance with plans. Proper backfill practices and finish grading are extremely important for keeping a foundation dry over the long term, and should be inspected and checked against specifications.
Roofing: during or just after roof sheathing is installed	Inspect roof sheathing installation in high-wind areas. Because underlayment is sometimes installed by the framing contractor immediately after completion of roof sheathing, a timely inspection of the sheathing for proper fastening is critical.
Roofing: prior to underlayment	Verify installation of eave ice-dam flashing 24 inches beyond exterior walls. For regions prone to ice dams, periodically inspect for the presence of ice-dam flashing, and ensure that it extends 24 inches horizontally beyond the plane of the exterior wall.
HVAC Rough-In	Inspect exhaust ducts. Check that exhaust ducts are vented to the outdoors and run in straight, direct lengths.
HVAC Rough-In	Inspect and/or test the central duct system. Verify that the central duct system is sealed with adequate materials at all joints.
HVAC Rough-In	Check for proper operation of the ventilation system. Operate the mechanical ventilation system to confirm that controls, dampers and other features work.
Plumbing Rough-In	Check that supplemental dehumidification equipment is plumbed to a drain. In cases where a permanent, supplemental dehumidification system is used, verify that it can be plumbed to a water drain line.
After Mechanical Rough-In	Check for adequate groundcover in the crawlspace. Once mechanical systems are installed, check that a continuous and lapped groundcover is installed in the crawlspace. The groundcover should not be torn.
Insulating and Air-Sealing	Inspect envelope air-sealing details. A quick visual inspection should be conducted to verify that major air-leakage areas are corrected. Blower-door testing can be performed by a professional before building assemblies are closed in to identify and address leakage points.
Insulation in Attic and Walls	Inspect wall and attic insulation. Confirm that insulated areas are free of voids and points of compressed insulation. Also, make sure that attic insulation does not cover eave vents, and that cathedral ceilings are insulated as specified.

Table 12: Construction-Phase Inspection	
Insulation R-Values	Confirm attic R-values when insulating for ice-dam prevention. Verify attic insulation R-value, especially when insulating beyond local code requirements for enhanced ice-dam prevention.
Basement Finishing	Confirm basement finishes for moisture resistance. Verify that basement wall gypsum is not in direct contact with the slab, and that insulation details meet specifications.
Occupancy	Provide clients with educational materials on moisture. As homeowners assume maintenance and operation of the home, it's critical for them to understand some moisture basics. Consider directing clients to this site: www.epa.gov/mold/moldguide.html

Part 4: Water Management and Damage Prevention

General

Designing, building and maintaining homes that manage moisture effectively comprise a process of good decision-making. While builders and designers provide most of the up-front decisions, such as designing the roof system and specifying the foundation's drainage details, over the long term, the homeowner must understand basic moisture issues and make good decisions at the right times.

This section provides homeowners with basic information to make these decisions and to take the appropriate actions to keep their homes dry and comfortable.

There is already plenty of useful guidance for homeowners on what to do (and what not to do) regarding moisture. Builders, housing groups, insurance organizations, and government agencies all have produced credible guidance on this topic. Therefore, this section of the book does not re-invent the wheel, but will instead rely on available guidance for homeowners. The tips that follow are based on information from the Insurance Institute for Business and Home Safety (IBHS) publication: *Is Your Home Protected from Water Damage?* The IBHS (**disastersafety.org** is a nonprofit association that engages in communication, education, engineering and research.

This section also includes inspection tips and recommendations that may help the inspector to spot common types of moisture problems in the home during an inspection. Most (if not all) moisture-related problems can become serious and expensive if not taken care of quickly and completely. Therefore, it is important for an inspector to call out or recommend further evaluations and/or repairs by qualified professionals when any moisture intrusion is discovered.

Moisture Control for Homeowners

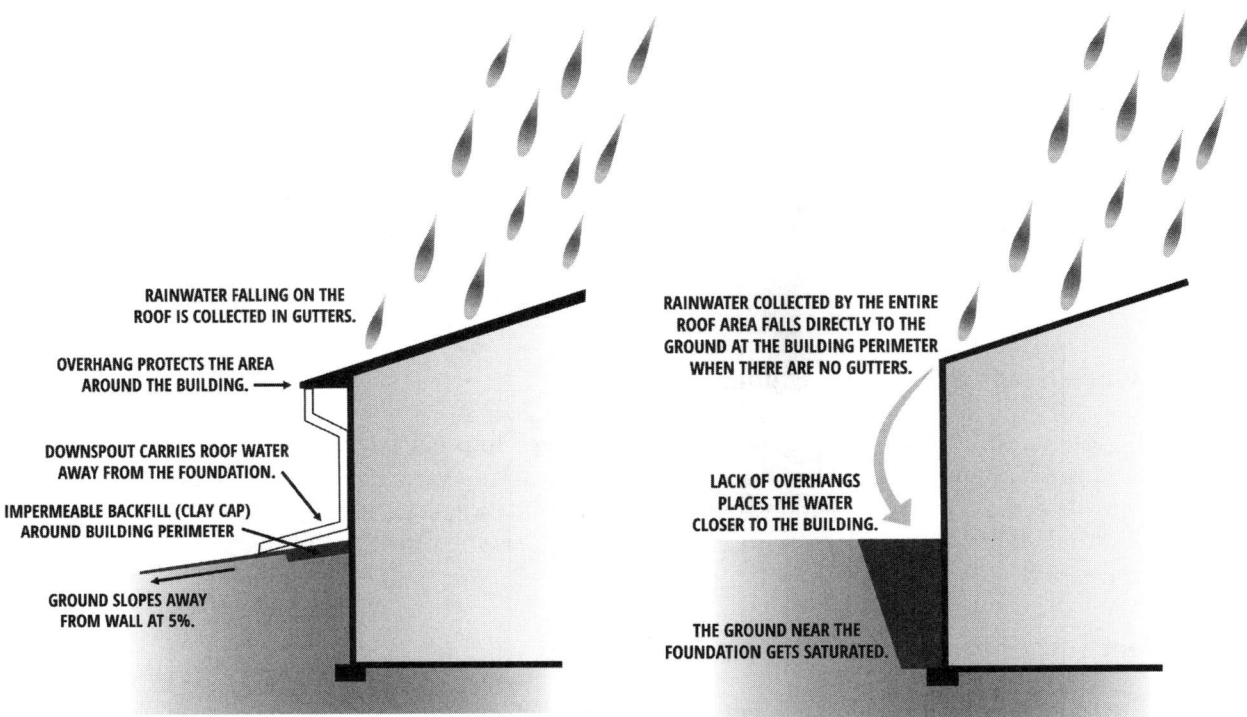

RAINWATER FALLING ON THE ROOF IS COLLECTED IN GUTTERS.

OVERHANG PROTECTS THE AREA AROUND THE BUILDING. ➞

DOWNSPOUT CARRIES ROOF WATER AWAY FROM THE FOUNDATION.

IMPERMEABLE BACKFILL (CLAY CAP) AROUND BUILDING PERIMETER

GROUND SLOPES AWAY FROM WALL AT 5%.

RAINWATER COLLECTED BY THE ENTIRE ROOF AREA FALLS DIRECTLY TO THE GROUND AT THE BUILDING PERIMETER WHEN THERE ARE NO GUTTERS.

LACK OF OVERHANGS PLACES THE WATER CLOSER TO THE BUILDING.

THE GROUND NEAR THE FOUNDATION GETS SATURATED.

Water, in all its forms, is an ever-present fact of life, especially for homeowners. Households commonly use and dispose of hundreds of gallons of tap water on a daily basis. Torrents of rainwater must be successfully shed by the roof and walls during thunderstorms. Groundwater travels through the soil beneath the foundation. We control indoor humidity levels for maximum comfort. The house itself absorbs and releases moisture in the forms of condensation and water vapor.

When a well-built home is properly maintained, water is a benefit and a pleasure. On the other hand, uncontrolled water in our homes can cause damage, expense, and considerable inconvenience. It can lead to mold growth, rotting wood, and structural damage. It can also lead to the loss of irreplaceable personal belongings.

How Your House Handles Water

Imagine your house as a living thing. It has multiple ways to resist, absorb and channel excess moisture, as needed, to maintain its well-being, comfort and safety.

Your House Repels Excess Water

The exterior surfaces of your house, from the roof to the foundation, make up its envelope or "skin." The skin is designed to shed or repel excess water. If it doesn't, expect trouble. When roof flashings, windows, foundation walls, and other building components are not properly maintained, rainwater will find its way into vulnerable parts of your house.

Your House Absorbs and Releases Excess Moisture

All houses must absorb and release moisture constantly in order to maintain a healthy balance. If your house has "breathing" problems, many types of moisture problems can develop. Trapped moisture — dampness that cannot be released, for one reason or another — is one of the primary causes of fungus and mold growth in a house. Fungi can literally eat wood, causing decay, rot, and, ultimately, structural damage. Trapped moisture in the walls can destroy the value of your insulation and, consequently, raise heating and cooling costs. Wood that stays moist attracts carpenter ants and other insects that can accelerate structural problems.

Your House Transports Piped Water

Directly beneath the skin of your house is a complex maze of pipes carrying fresh water into your house, and drain lines to dispose of water after its use. There are dozens of pipe joints and specialized fittings throughout your house, any one of which can develop a leak and cause moisture damage.

Your House Needs a Firm, Dry Foundation

The best foundation is a dry foundation. A water-damaged foundation is extremely expensive to repair and can lead to damage in the rest of the house. Groundwater, floodwater, and even rainwater from a misdirected downspout can undermine your foundation and cause settling cracks and wet floors and walls, and lead to conditions that can support the growth of undesirable bio-matter, including mold.

Frequent Causes of Moisture Damage

Unwanted water can intrude through cracks in the protective skin of your house. It can also accumulate from interior moisture sources. The most common causes of both types of moisture problems are covered in this section.

Roof and Flashing Problems

Roofing materials can wear out, break, rust, blow off, or otherwise fail and expose the roof deck and structural components beneath to moisture intrusion and damage.

Most leaks occur around penetrations through the roof, such as at a chimney, plumbing vent, exhaust fan, and skylight. Flashings and sealant joints around these penetrations can crack, fail and leak. Intersections of roof surfaces at walls are also common leakage points.

Old and defective shingles can curl and crack, allowing moisture intrusion. If old shingles aren't removed before new roof shingles are applied, they can reduce the life of the new roof. Chimney caps can crack, allowing water into interior areas of the chimney.

Shingle edges can fail, forcing rainwater to accumulate between the roof and gutter.

Flat or low-pitched roofs have unique maintenance needs and are susceptible to water problems because they may not drain as quickly as roofs with a steeper pitch.

Flat roof drains and scuppers can clog and hold water on the roof, increasing the risk not only of a leak but of a possible collapse of the entire roof under the weight of the water.

Gutter and Downspout Problems

Clogged gutters can force rainwater to travel up onto the roof and under shingles. It can overflow and travel down the inside of the wall. It can overflow and collect at the home's foundation.

First-floor gutters can overflow if second-floor gutters have been mistakenly directed to drain into them.

An insufficient number of downspouts and undersized downspouts can cause gutters to overflow.

Downspouts that don't empty far enough away from foundation walls can lead to foundation wall damage and a wet basement.

Ice Dams

Inadequate attic insulation allows heat to escape from the house into the attic, which can turn rooftop snow into an ice dam along the eaves. Ice dams frequently force moisture to back up under the roof shingles where it can drip into the attic or walls.

Clogged or frozen gutters can act like ice dams, pushing moisture up under the shingles and into the house.

Soffits and Fasciae Can Become Damaged

Damaged soffits (horizontal surfaces under the eaves) can allow snow and rain to be blown into the attic, damaging the insulation, ceilings and walls.

Fascia boards (vertical roof-trim sections) can become damaged, allowing the moisture from rain and snow into the attic and atop interior walls.

Weep Holes Can Become Clogged

Weep holes, which are designed to allow moisture to escape from behind walls, can become blocked.

Weep holes can freeze, forcing moisture to back up inside the wall cavity.

Weep holes can become clogged with landscape mulch, soil and other material.

Landscape Grade Changes Can Occur

Recent landscaping modifications may result in water drainage back toward the foundation, rather than away from it.

A newly built home lot may have been graded improperly, or the original foundation backfill may have settled over time, causing drainage problems.

Automatic sprinklers may be spraying water onto or too close to the foundation walls.

Window and Door Flashing and Seals May Need Repair

Cracked, torn and damaged seals, weatherstripping, and flashing around windows and doors can allow wind-blown moisture to penetrate your house.

Improperly installed windows and doors can allow moisture into the wall.

Worn or failed weatherstripping can allow wind-driven rain to penetrate a closed window or door.

Groundwater and Rainwater Collecting

During wet seasons, groundwater and misdirected rainwater can collect along the foundation wall or beneath the floor or slab. Unless it is directed away from the structure by a sump pump or corrected drainage, this moisture can lead to mold growth, wall failure, and other destructive moisture problems.

If Plumbing Develops Slow or Catastrophic Leaks

Plumbing fixtures, including dishwashers, disposals, toilets, sinks, water heaters, showers, clothes washers, tubs and other enclosures, can have pipe-joint or hose-attachment failures and develop leaks, or hoses can rupture.

Leaks inside walls may go undetected for some time and result in significant damage.

Kitchen appliances, such as a refrigerator, icemaker or dishwasher, can develop water line leaks.

Metal piping can corrode internally or be damaged externally.

Hanging heavy items from pipes can cause a leak or failure.

Drains can clog and cause water to back up into the house.

The water heater can have a slow leak, or fail catastrophically, causing flooding.

Condensation Can Form on Windows, Pipes and Inside Walls

Condensation on windows can, at a minimum, damage window sills and finishes. At worst, it can damage walls and floors, as well.

Condensation on uninsulated pipes can collect nearby or travel along a pipe to accumulate far from the original source.

Condensation can form inside improperly built walls and lead to serious water damage and biological growth that are hidden from sight.

Heating and Air-Conditioning Systems Need Maintenance

Lapses in regular maintenance can lead to moisture and comfort problems, ranging from clogged drain pans to iced-up cooling coils and mold within the system.

Failure to clean and service air conditioners regularly can lead to diminishing performance, higher operating costs, and potential moisture problems.

Humidifiers can add too much moisture to a house, leading to dampness and mold.

Sump Pumps Need Maintenance or Replacement

Neglecting to test a sump pump routinely — especially if it is rarely used — can lead to severe water damage, especially when a heavy storm, snow melt or flooding sends water against the home.

Overload of the sump pump due to poor drainage elsewhere on the property can lead to pump failure. Frequent sump operation can be a sign of excessive water buildup under the basement floor. This can be due to poorly sloped landscaping, poor rain runoff, gutter back-flows, and other problems.

Lack of a backup sump pump, which can be quickly activated in the event the first pump fails, can lead to serious water damage and property loss. This is especially important if you rely heavily on your sump pump to maintain a dry basement, or if you live in an area of seasonally high groundwater. Sump failure can cause extensive water damage and the loss of valuable personal belongings.

Where to Look for Problems

An "ounce of prevention" can prevent "gallons" of potential water leaks and damage — and a regular maintenance program is the easiest way to protect a home and its contents. The following checklists, organized room by room, describe early warning signs to help prevent (or at least minimize) water-related problems and moisture damage. Testing or operating kitchen and laundry appliances is beyond the scope of a typical home inspection, although many home inspectors will turn on the appliances during the inspection.

What to Look for in the Kitchen

It is easy to overlook the warning signs of excess moisture and impending water damage. Learn to keep an eye out for these all-too-common sources of moisture damage.

Under the Kitchen Sink

Under the sink is not just for storage and the trash can. It is often the starting point for many water-related problems. Dampness and musty odors are common signs of a leak.

Is a drip in the trap under the sink going unnoticed? It's a warning sign of potentially serious drain problems.

Is a steady drip at a faucet going unnoticed? Recommend that it be repaired promptly.

Are there damp or stained areas in or under the wall where the plumbing pipes penetrate?

Are there large holes in the wall with smaller pipes coming through? These holes should be filled with appropriate foams, caulks and sealants.

Is the floor beneath the plumbing penetrations soft or stained?

Around the Kitchen Sink

The kitchen sink is a high-traffic zone that sees more action than almost any other place in the home.

Is the backsplash cracked? Are the sink seals cracked or loose?

Is the countertop tile or grout cracked, broken or missing? Although it may appear to be only a minor cosmetic issue, it's not a minor issue when it comes to moisture control.

Under the Dishwasher

This workhorse appliance is often overlooked as a water-damage risk.

Most inspectors turn on and operate the dishwasher in order to look for failures in operation.

If the dishwasher backs up or overflows into the sink, there may be a clogged drain line. The drain line should be cleaned regularly.

If the dishwasher fails to completely empty after use, the main filter and drain may be clogged.

Find a small leak in the dishwasher water supply hose? It needs to be replaced immediately.

Behind the Refrigerator

We rarely inspect behind the refrigerator. But a check-up may prevent messy problems. If the refrigerator has an icemaker, check for damage or disconnection of the supply line.

Moisture behind the refrigerator is a big red flag. Even if you can diagnose the source of the problem, call out for a professional. Don't ignore even a slight leak or kink in the icemaker's supply line.

If unidentifiable moldy objects are growing underneath the refrigerator, call them out. There shouldn't be any moisture under the refrigerator.

If the model has a drain pan, check the pan for cleanliness and bacterial or mold growth.

Beneath the Cooking Range

Open the bottom drawer to inspect underneath the stove. You may see signs of moisture or mold.

Kitchen Exhaust Fans and Filters

Fans and filters are small items that play a big role in moisture and mold management. Some fans merely filter and re-circulate air, which does not reduce moisture produced from cooking.

Is the range exhaust filter caked and dirty?

Is the exhaust fan covered with dust?

If there are down-vented indoor grills, check them. They should be clean to ensure the free flow of air.

Bathroom Problems: What to Look For

Plumbing

Most plumbing is hidden in the walls, and serious problems can begin "invisibly."

Listen for tiny drips in the wall.

If a wall is damp to the touch or discolored, there is moisture damage in progress.

Any visible leaks under the sink or around the toilet need to be fixed before they lead to more serious and expensive moisture damage.

Signs of water damage in flooring in the bathroom, or on the ceilings of rooms below a bathroom, are a red flag of a possible water leak.

Exhaust Fan

One of the most important tools for moisture management in the bathroom is the exhaust fan.

A non-functioning exhaust fan overloads the bathroom with damp air.

If the exhaust fan doesn't come on automatically when the bathroom light is turned on, consider recommending a wiring or switch change so that the fan will activate simultaneously with the light. A switch can also be installed that turns on the fan when the bathroom humidity is high, or that uses a timer switch that will operate the fan for 30 to 40 minutes after a shower.

Be certain that the bathroom exhaust fan vents to the outdoors, and not into the house or attic.

Toilet

The toilet has critical inlet and outlet functions that need to be sealed so that they're leak-free.

Make sure there are no leaks in the water line.

Check for signs of staining and water damage on the floor. If present, immediately check the toilet rim seal and tank seal. If the toilet rocks back and forth when pushed slightly (using your leg), the floor drain may not be sealed properly to the toilet.

If the floor around the toilet seems soft or seems to give, structural damage may be occurring.

Windows

Bathroom windows need to perform properly in a wide range of humidity and temperature conditions.

Check to see if there are any obvious breaks in the weatherstripping or seals.

Are there are stains or flaking on the painted surfaces?

Showers and Bathtubs

Areas that are exposed to this much water need close inspection.

Is the caulking cracked, stiff or loose in spots?

Are there cracked tiles or missing grout that may channel water to vulnerable areas?

If some water remains in the bathtub after draining, it may be a warning sign of possible structural weakening and settlement in the floor beneath the tub.

Inspecting the Utility Room

What to Look For

The water heater and the heating, ventilation and cooling (HVAC) system may be located anywhere, from the attic to the basement, or in a utility room. Regardless of the location, here are some concerns you can address while inspecting for moisture damage and moisture-related problems.

Water Heater

The tank should be clean and rust-free. If you find rust developing, it is often a sign of imminent tank failure. Recommend that it be checked immediately because the old water heater may need replacing.

Check for any tiny leaks at the inlet and outlet pipes. First, turn off the water and power supply.

The area around the tank should be clean and dry. If you find signs of dampness, investigate or call for further evaluation.

The bottom drain valve should be dry and rust-free. If you see rust, check for leaks around the valve.

If the tank is gas-fired, confirm that the exhaust vent and shield are in place and functioning properly. Call for a professional if you suspect any problem, as malfunctioning water heater units can cause life-threatening conditions.

Water Softener

The area around the tank should be clean and dry. If there are signs of moisture, check for leaks.

Heating Systems

If the furnace burns oil or gas products, proper ventilation of combustion gases is essential. Call for a professional if you suspect any problem, as malfunctioning heating systems can cause life-threatening conditions.

Because most gas-heating systems also generate water during combustion, proper ventilation and periodic maintenance of the furnace will help ensure that the water is properly vented and drained away. Look for recent service records.

Recommend changing the HVAC system filters monthly in order to help reduce dust and pollutants in the home, as well as limit any sort of growth that might start there.

Check that all through-the-wall penetrations for fuel lines, ducts, and electrical systems are well-sealed.

All ducts should be clean and dust-free. Inspect the air-supply registers in the house for dust accumulation.

Duct installation and sealing ducts in unconditioned spaces, such as an attic and crawlspace, should be insulated. Recommend that gaps and holes be sealed with foil-backed tape or mastic.

Cooling Systems

Filters, supply lines, exterior wall penetrations, vents, ductwork, and drainage systems must all be in good working order to avoid moisture problems.

Call out for regular inspection and cleaning of the cooling drainage pan. The drainage pan operation is very important because water removal is a key element of the cooling system's operation.

At season switchover, recommend the removal of dust and particulates that may have settled in the drainage pan over the winter.

Recommend hiring a professional to look at the heat exchanger when servicing the cooling unit.

If the air conditioner coils ice up, or if the A/C runs all the time, it can be a sign of several problems. Besides not working properly, these issues can also cause water accumulation and mold within the system.

Other HVAC Systems

Whole-house fans, humidifiers, dehumidifiers, evaporative coolers, radon mitigation systems, and other indoor air-quality systems need periodic check-ups.

Attempt to determine whether the dehumidifier has a clogged or clear drain. The cooling coils should be cleaned regularly.

Through-the-roof penetrations require careful inspection for water intrusion-related issues. Radon mitigation and HVAC systems, attic fans, and whole-house fans must be checked to confirm that flashings and sealants are in good condition. Check framing and sheathing around these penetrations for signs of staining and water intrusion. If you can see daylight, it may be evidence of a problem.

Through-the-wall penetrations should be handled with as much care as through-the-roof penetrations. Electrical, plumbing, HVAC, communications, home security, cable, exhaust vents, and pet doors can become sources of serious moisture intrusion. Inspect them carefully.

Recommend regularly checking the filters, watering pad, reservoir, pump and water connections of an evaporative cooler. Hard water can damage these systems. Annual reservoir de-mineralizing treatments and pad replacement are important.

Recommend checking the water connections, and clean the evaporator pad of a whole-house humidifier monthly. At the end of each heating season, the pads should be replaced to prevent unwanted biological growth.

Utility Room Tips

Carbon-monoxide detectors are one way to help in the early detection of combustion gas problems. Recommend to your clients to install these detectors.

Your clients will save money on their utility bills if the heat exchanger and cooling coils in the air conditioner and heat pumps are clean and dust-free.

Monthly replacement of HVAC filters saves money on heating and cooling costs, as well as reduces the potential of moisture-related growth.

Keeping all ductwork well-taped and sealed is still another way to achieve home energy-cost savings.

At the time of seasonal switchover, drains that do not flow freely should be cleaned. They can be flushed with hot water and a few tablespoons of bleach.

Kitchen, bath and other exhaust fans should be cleaned of dirt and debris regularly (such as birds' nests) from indoors and outdoors.

Wall penetrations for the heating and cooling systems should all be well-sealed and insulated.

What to Look for When Inspecting the Attic

Roof Pass-Throughs and Penetrations

You should invest in a moisture meter to use on your inspections.

Inspect each location at which something passes through the roof. These typically include chimneys, plumbing vent pipes, skylight wells, radon vents, etc. If any of the following warning signs are present, recommend a qualified professional.

Does anything appear wet? Are there stains on the wood? This is a telltale sign of a previous leak. Is the surface at the stain still damp or cool to the touch?

Is there a musty smell?

Are there any visible signs of mold or rot?

Attic Vents

In most houses, vents are installed near gables, eaves, at the soffits, and along the peak of the roof. Proper attic ventilation is very important.

Is the wood and insulation near the vents dry? Dampness or surface discoloration may be a warning sign of moisture penetration.

Check that all vents are securely attached to the walls and roof and are not loose.

Check for any birds' nests, insulation, or other debris blocking the vents.

Look Down!

Be sure to look down, as well as up, when checking for moisture damage in the attic.

Insulation

Is the insulation still looking soft and fluffy? Is it thick?

If there are areas that look unusually thin or flattened, it could be a sign of moisture damage. Feel and measure the area for moisture.

If insulation near the eaves and soffits is not as fluffy and thick as it is near the middle, it could be a sign of a damaged soffit or other perimeter leak. Be sure the insulation does not cover soffit vents. Air needs to be able to flow through the vents.

Examine ceiling penetrations coming up from the space below, such as plumbing vent stacks and ducts. These penetrations should be sealed against air leakage with appropriate materials.

HVAC Systems in the Attic

Attic HVAC systems and ductwork can be sources of unwanted moisture intrusion. Inspect the ductwork. Are the duct joints exposed or not properly sealed? If the insulation surrounding the ductwork is deteriorating, call it out in your report.

Recessed Lights

You can often spot clues of the presence of excessive attic moisture around these fixtures.

Inspect all lighting canisters. If the canisters show rust or corrosion, it could be a warning sign of a potential electrical hazard, in addition to possible moisture intrusion.

If the wood and insulation around the canisters are stained or show color differences, it is a clear sign of unwanted moisture. Check above and around these areas for sources of moisture.

Walls Connecting the Attic to the Basement

Interior partition walls that go from the attic to the basement are often used for electrical, plumbing and ductwork chases that can contain hidden moisture problems.

If insulation is missing in the middle of the attic, there may be unwanted air flow from the basement to the attic through an interior partition. Recommend that these types of hidden channels get sealed off and insulated to prevent air and moisture flow.

Attic Tips

When checking or adding attic insulation, be sure that none of the soffit vents is covered or blocked.

Make recommendations to conduct attic checks routinely in the summer and in the winter. Many moisture problems are seasonal.

Stains near attic vents are signs of previous moisture intrusion through or around these vents. The cause should be investigated promptly, even if the area is currently dry.

Remember to treat an attic air-conditioning drain exactly as you would any other household drain. Routine maintenance should include a periodic removal of dust and debris, followed by a flush of hot water and bleach.

Squirrels, mice, bats, snakes and other rodents and small animals often get into attics through small defects in soffits and vents. They can do additional damage that can lead to moisture problems.

Basement Moisture Problems

What to Look For

Basements often contain a wide array of the plumbing, electrical, HVAC, communications, waste removal, and other systems of the home, which means there are plenty of potential moisture problems. Here's what you should recommend that the homeowner keep an eye on.

All Basements

Sometimes, clues found in the basement can lead to the discovery of a leak in a bathroom or attic, or even a clogged gutter.

Look for water trails and stains on the basement walls and on the floor above. Investigate the sources of all such stains or trails.

Water pipes can sweat, and this condensation, if left uncontrolled, can result in mold growth, mustiness, rust and rot. Look for pipes with beads of moisture on them. Insulating all pipes reduces condensation and saves on energy bills.

If the heating and/or air-conditioning system is in the basement, check the drain pan and filter. If the drain pan has collected dust and debris, or does not drain freely, clean and flush the drain. Filters need regular cleaning and periodic replacement.

Look at All HVAC Ductwork

Inspect all overhead floor penetrations from drains and other systems. If there is any evidence of moisture around these penetrations, or if they are not well-sealed, check the source of the moisture.

Check all basement vents, including the laundry, water heater and furnace vents, and radon and bathroom exhaust fans, for any signs of faulty operation. Vent failure is serious and should be repaired by a professional.

Check the sump pump, if there is one. If the pump frequently switches on and off, there may be excessive water build-up under the basement floor or slab.

In basements that are going to be finished for additional living space, any signs of moisture — whether they're continual or only seasonal — must be addressed before the space is finished. The use of a supplemental dehumidifier in basements is a good idea if the area is damp, and it can also be used to help the basement in a new house dry out over the first couple of years after construction.

Crawlspaces

Damp crawlspaces are likely places for unwanted moisture and mold growth.

Be sure that exterior grading does not slope toward the foundation walls.

All crawlspaces should have a plastic groundcover to block moisture from the ground, and to prevent mold growth and structural damage.

Unfinished Basements

Even these types of basements should remain dry.

If basement walls or floors are wet, investigate further. Try to determine the source of the moisture, or recommend further evaluation.

If there is insulation on the walls or floors, inspect to see if it is dry and in good condition.

Check the floor drain, if there is one.

Basement Tips

Damp basements attract pests, such as cockroaches, mice, snakes, etc., especially during the heat of summer. A basement should remain cool, dry and clean.

Test the sump pump to be sure that it functions properly. Try pouring some water into the sump chamber and test to see if the float switch turns the motor on and that the pump drains the chamber.

If the pump is relied on heavily to maintain dry conditions in the basement, the owner should consider purchasing a backup pump that could be quickly activated in the event that the first pump fails. Sump failure can cause extensive damage from an otherwise harmless rainstorm.

A backup power supply system for the pump may be considered.

Laundry Room Moisture Problems

What to Look For

The recurring cycle of warmth, moisture and lint in laundry rooms can invite all sorts of problems. Here are a few warning signs and regular maintenance steps you can offer to prevent them.

Washing Machine Connections

Inspect for tiny leaks in the connections to both hot and cold water lines.

Check both ends of the water lines for possible leaks.

Check the discharge hose for kinks and cracks. If the hose is brittle or old, it should be replaced.

Hard Water Problems

In areas with mineral-laden or "hard" water where the washer is slow to fill, there's a good chance that the in-line filter is clogged.

Is there a steady drip into the washing machine? Grit has probably damaged the shut-off valve.

Utility Sinks

If the utility sink drains sluggishly, there could be blockage in the drain line.

Watch for any signs of dripping faucets, water damage to the flooring, and leaks in the drainpipe.

Dryer Connections

If the dryer vent hose isn't tightly connected to the outside vent, repair to the clamp is needed.

Mechanical fasteners, such clamps, are more effective and appropriate than tape.

If dryer lint has accumulated behind and under the dryer, the vent pipe may be clogged. Check to see if it is free of debris both from the inside and outside of the house.

If there are too many twists and turns in the line for the dryer to vent efficiently, make the exhaust shorter and straighter, taking care that it still terminates to the outside.

What to Look for Outside

Exterior Sidings and Wall Penetrations

Are siding boards cracked or broken? Is the vinyl cracked? Is building paper or structural sheathing visible?

Cracks in brick, stucco, stone and other masonry need further investigation.

Check weep holes. Clean holes prevent trapping water behind walls.

Damaged exterior hose bibs that have even slight leaks need repair.

Any open or unsealed exterior wall penetrations, such as those for wiring, plumbing, telephone, cable and HVAC lines, should be re-sealed with appropriate caulk, foam or sealant.

If exhaust vent doors no longer close snugly against their gaskets, they need repair.

Inspect seals along the wall openings around vents and other penetrations.

Look for any exposed, unstained or unpainted wood surrounding wall penetrations.

Look for signs of termite infestation or moisture intrusion from earlier termite damage.

Windows and Doors

Do the closed windows still show cracks between the sash and frame? Are they difficult to open and close?

Is any window flashing loose or damaged?

Are the perimeter sealants no longer pliable and continuous?

Are there signs of moisture accumulation above or under the windows? Check all water management systems above the windows, including shingles, gutters, flashing, siding and soffit vents.

Are there doors that no longer fit tightly, or locks that do not hold the door tightly against the seals?

Is the weatherstripping between the window sash cracked, or has it worn away completely? Weatherstripping in good condition is vital to prevent both water and air leakage.

Good Drainage

Has the ground settled or sloped toward the foundation?

Do any downspouts discharge near the house?

Do the gutter drains slope toward the house? Make sure they slope away from the house.

Has the landscaping altered the water drainage? Landscaping should promote positive drainage away from the foundation.

Does the driveway channel water toward the house? Re-grading or altering the drainage to carry driveway water away from the foundation may be needed.

Trees

Tree roots and yard pests can clog drain lines to septic fields and other water management systems.

If any limbs are so close to the roof that they could be holding moisture against the shingles, they should be trimmed or removed.

If tree limbs brush against the house or windows during high winds or thunderstorms, they should be trimmed to prevent possible damage to the siding, shingles, gutters and windows.

Walk around the perimeter of the house during an inspection to see where gutters, downspouts and drainage systems may not be performing adequately.

Check for Roof Moisture Problems

What to Look For

Shingles

Are the shingles worn, curled or missing?

If the gutters are filled up with shingle grit, it's a sign of rapid aging and should be investigated further.

On a tiled roof, any visibly cracked or missing tiles should be repaired or replaced.

On a wood shingle or shake roof, look for curled, deteriorated or mossy shingles. Moss may be a sign of insufficient water drainage and should be inspected by a professional roofer. Recommend that any damaged or missing shakes be replaced.

Older rooftop antennae can literally drill holes in shingles. Check the feet of any antennae.

Flashing

Performing an on-the-roof inspection is best to assess flashing quality and any damage.

If the chimney flashing doesn't appear smooth and intact, it needs closer inspection.

If the flashing and sealants have failed and there are obvious holes in the sheathing or even penetrating into the attic, recommend further evaluation and correction.

Check that the perimeter of any skylight is well-flashed and sealed.

Check the shingles around the skylights. If any shingles are curled or cracked, recommend calling a professional roofer.

Check the flashing and seals on all plumbing stack vents, chimneys, skylights, and other roof penetrations.

Gutters

Most gutter checks should be conducted from the safety of a ladder on the ground. But if you can safely access the roof, take a quick look into the gutters.

If the shingle drip edge (the metal strip under the first course of shingles above the gutter) is damaged or missing, or if the shingle edges have cracked and fallen into the gutter, the edge needs prompt repair.

If you can see an excessive amount of shingle grit or granules in the gutters, it is not only a sign of shingle aging, but the grit can also impede the flow of water out of the gutter.

If the gutters frequently fill with leaves and twigs, recommend purchasing gutter shields that allow water in while keeping leaves and other debris out.

If there is standing water in the gutters, the slope of the gutter may need adjustment to ensure proper draining to the downspouts.

Membrane Roofs

Flat roofs can create serious water problems if not maintained properly.

If you see standing water on the roof, recommend having the roof inspected further by a professional roofer.

Are the roof drains clogged?

Are there visible cracks in the membrane?

All of these issues require maintenance and possibly further mitigation, repair or replacement.

Quiz #5

1. _____-cycling of the central air-conditioning system reduces energy efficiency and can decrease the moisture vapor or latent heat-removal capability of conventional A/C equipment by as much as one-half.

    ☐ Multi

    ☐ Short

    ☐ Over

    ☐ Long

2. Building codes require that joints in duct systems be made "substantially" _____ by means of tapes, mastics, gaskets, or other approved methods.

    ☐ airtight

    ☐ loose

    ☐ restricted

    ☐ open

3. T/F: In addition to alleviating pressure imbalances and limiting air leakage through the building envelope, sealing duct leakage can also improve comfort and eliminate carpet soiling problems, which can leave darkened stains on the perimeter of carpets.

    ☐ True

    ☐ False

4. T/F: Inspectors should recommend that all exhaust vents be directly vented to the outside by attachment of exhaust vent ducting to appropriate through-wall or through-roof ventilation hoods.

    ☐ True

    ☐ False

5. T/F: Inspectors are often hired to oversee each phase of the construction of a new home.

    ☐ True

    ☐ False

6. T/F: Home inspectors are required to inspect for code-compliance.

    ☐ True

    ☐ False

Answer Key is on page 118.

Part 5: In Conclusion

To review, this publication covers: moisture-resistant roof systems; moisture-resistant exterior walls, including flashing at doors and windows; moisture-resistant foundations, including insulating crawlspaces, slab-on-grade, and finished basements; ground clearances; moisture vapor control; humidity; air leakage; and vapor retarders.

That's a lot to know about inspecting for moisture intrusion. But building practices and construction techniques are essential for an inspector to understand. Building components that are defective, incorrectly installed, or simply missing can produce moisture-related problems. Moisture intrusion into a building can cause major structural damage and can threaten the safety of its occupants. When an inspector knows what a properly installed building component looks like, then recognizing an installation defect is easy. Education and training on the best and most recent building practices for controlling moisture are essential for every property inspector.

A well-constructed and well-maintained home can protect the occupants, increase their comfort, and lower their energy and repair costs.

Appendix I: Answer Keys

Answer Key for Quiz #1

1. Moisture and water vapor move in and out of a house in three ways: with air currents; by diffusion through materials; and by **heat** transfer.

2. Of the three main ways that moisture moves through a house, **air** movement accounts for more than 98% of all water vapor movement in building cavities.

3. **Relative humidity (RH)** refers to the amount of moisture contained in a quantity of air compared to the maximum amount of moisture the air could hold at the same temperature.

4. T/F: Roof coverings provide the first line of defense against the elements and tend to be the most exposed components of a building's exterior envelope.
Answer: **True**

5. The minimum pitch for a composition-shingle roof is **2:12**.

6. For roof slopes of 2:12 to 4:12, there should be **two** layers of underlayment applied.

7. Re-roofing over an existing layer of composition shingles, while generally permitted by code, reduces the ability of the newer shingles to resist impact damage from **hail**.

8. T/F: Roofing cement and caulk are adequate substitutes for general flashing details in order to prevent roof leaks.
Answer: **False**

Answer Key for Quiz #2

1. Roof system ventilation and insulation are important for a number of reasons: condensation control; temperature control; energy efficiency; and prevention of chronic **ice**-dam formation.

2. Roof **overhangs** and projections provide a primary means of deflecting rainwater away from building walls.

3. A **water-resistive barrier** is one layer of 15-pound asphalt felt applied over the studs or sheathing of all exterior walls.

4. T/F: Caulking of nail flanges (particularly at the window head and jambs) is critical to the prevention of moisture intrusion around commonly used nail-flange windows.
Answer: **True**

5. T/F: A drained-cavity WRE relies on deflection, drainage and drying to protect the wall from moisture damage.
Answer: **True**

6. **Flashing** at exterior window and door openings shall extend to the surface of the exterior wall finish, or to the water-resistive barrier, for subsequent drainage.

7. T/F: Approved corrosion-resistant flashings shall be installed continuously above all projecting wood trim.
Answer: **True**

8. T/F: In general, caulks and sealants should be relied on as the primary means of defense against water intrusion at joints in a WRE system.
Answer: **False**

9. T/F: Silicone rubber and urethane caulks generally give the best overall performance for exterior building envelope applications.
Answer: **True**

10. T/F: Model building standards typically require a minimum of 6-inch of fall in ground level over a distance of 10 feet from the perimeter of the building.
Answer: **True**

11. T/F: A condition that is beyond the scope of an inspector's consideration on a building site includes a high local water table (within 4 to 8 feet of the lowest proposed foundation floor grade level).
Answer: **False**

12. T/F: Poor site drainage of surface water is perhaps the most important contributor to a foundation's moisture problems.
Answer: **True**

13. The upper layers of a **backfill** should be of moderate, low-permeability soil (with some clay content) to help reduce the direct infiltration of rainwater adjacent to the foundation.

14. Generally speaking, current model building codes require that **drains** be provided around all foundations that enclose habitable space (such as basements).

15. Model building codes typically require **damp-proofing** of foundation walls that retain earth and enclose interior spaces and floors below grade.

16. **Waterproofing** is the application of a combination of sealing materials and impervious coatings to prevent the passage of moisture in either a vapor or liquid form under conditions of significant hydrostatic pressure.

17. A(n) **epoxy** sealant can be injected into cracks of masonry foundation walls to stop water intrusion.

Answer Key for Quiz #3

1. T/F: Any successful basement finish design requires that exterior waterproofing, relative humidity control in the basement, and air-sealing are properly addressed.
Answer: **True**

2. For some climates, low-permeability and continuous vapor retarders on the **interior** side of basement finishes, such as polyethylene sheeting or vinyl wallpaper, should be avoided because they tend to trap moisture vapor moving through the foundation.

3. T/F: The fire and smoke characteristics of semi-permeable, rigid foam insulation on the inside of a basement foundation wall require that it be covered with a fire-resistant layer, such as gypsum.
Answer: **True**

4. If significant interior air leaks into an attic, **ventilation** may not be sufficient to prevent moisture and condensation problems in the attic.

5. T/F: In finished basements, finishes and baseboard trim should be held up about 1/2-inch from the slab surface.
Answer: **True**

6. The elevation of a slab-on-grade foundation (thickened-edge slab or independent slab and stem-wall foundation) should be a minimum of **8 inches** above the exterior finish grade.

7. A vapor barrier (such as 6-mil poly) or other approved **vapor retarder** is generally required, by standards, below any slab intended as a floor for habitable space.

8. T/F: Ideally, the best location for insulation in slab-on-grade foundations is on the vertical, outside face of the foundation.
Answer: **True**

9. T/F: Carpet and wood-based floor finishes should not be applied directly to slabs on grade unless the slab or finish surface temperature is raised near room temperature.
Answer: **True**

10. T/F: If a basement concrete floor slab shows signs of a pre-existing moisture problem, such as dampness or condensation, salt deposition, or standing water, the issue should be addressed after installing the finish flooring.
Answer: **False**

11. The top causes of moisture problems in crawlspaces include poor **site** drainage, lack of a ground vapor **barrier**, and crawlspace ventilation during humid summer conditions.

12. T/F: If the crawlspace elevation is below the exterior finish grade, foundation drainage and foundation wall damp-proofing should be provided in a fashion similar to that required for basements.
Answer: **True**

13. T/F: It is not necessary to vent a crawlspace for moisture control if it is open to an adjacent basement.
Answer: **True**

Answer Key for Quiz #4

1. Decay of common wood framing materials can begin when the moisture content of untreated wood exceeds **20%**.

2. One of the oldest and most trustworthy practices used to prevent wood and other moisture-sensitive materials from decaying is **separation from** a constant uptake of moisture from the ground.

3. T/F: The use of CCA (chromated copper arsenate) has been discontinued as a wood treatment except in certain commercial and agricultural applications.
Answer: **True**

4. T/F: A vapor retarder is defined as having < 1 perm based on a scale of permeance levels common to building codes and other industry literature.
Answer: **True**

5. T/F: High indoor humidity is a primary cause of many vapor-related moisture problems in homes.
   Answer: **True**

6. T/F: On a home construction site, it is acceptable for wood products to be stored in direct contact with the ground.
   Answer: **False**

7. **Air** leakage through building assemblies can move large quantities of water vapor and is a major factor in many vapor-related moisture problems.

8. T/F: Leakage of humid indoor air into cold cathedral roof cavities is a major cause of condensation and moisture problems.
   Answer: **True**

9. T/F: Air flow can transfer moisture vapor through and into building assemblies in amounts 10 to 100 times more than that which would typically occur by vapor diffusion.
   Answer: **True**

10. When installed incorrectly, vapor retarders can trap **moisture**, slow the normal drying process, and contribute to **moisture** damage.

11. T/F: In cold climates, exterior wall systems should dry toward the outside by locating vapor-retarding materials on the inside of the wall assembly, and making sure that exterior materials are vapor-permeable.
    Answer: **True**

Answer Key for Quiz #5

1. **Short**-cycling of the central air-conditioning system reduces energy efficiency and can decrease the moisture vapor or latent heat-removal capability of conventional A/C equipment by as much as one-half.

2. Building codes require that joints in duct systems be made "substantially" **airtight** by means of tapes, mastics, gaskets, or other approved methods.

3. T/F: In addition to alleviating pressure imbalances and limiting air leakage through the building envelope, sealing duct leakage can also improve comfort and eliminate carpet soiling problems, which can leave darkened stains on the perimeter of carpets.
   Answer: **True**

4. T/F: Inspectors should recommend that all exhaust vents be directly vented to the outside by attachment of exhaust vent ducting to appropriate through-wall or through-roof ventilation hoods.
   Answer: **True**

5. T/F: Inspectors are often hired to oversee each phase of the construction of a new home.
   Answer: **True**

6. T/F: Home inspectors are required to inspect for code-compliance.
   Answer: **False**

EDUCATION & TRAINING BOOKS

Whether you're new to the business, an inspector seeking more information, or a veteran of the industry looking to expand your knowledge, these official InterNACHI publications will help you become the best inspector you can be.

We Offer the Following Education & Training Books:

- **How to Inspect the Exterior**
  Item Number: 0094

- **How to Perform Deck Inspections**
  Item Number: 0029

- **Residential Plumbing Overview**
  Item Number: 0064

- **Inspecting HVAC Systems**
  Item Number: 0061

- **Safe Practices for the Home Inspector**
  Item Number: 0038

- **Inspecting the Attic, Insulation, Ventilation & Interior**
  Item Number: 0109

- **How to Perform Electrical Inspections**
  Item Number: 0023

- **How to Inspect Pools & Spas**
  Item Number: 0076

- **How to Perform Roof Inspections**
  Item Number: 0042

- **How to Perform a Mold Inspection**
  Item Number: 0022

- **How to Perform Radon Inspections**
  Item Number: 0028

- **Inspecting Foundation Walls and Piers**
  Item Number: 0065

- **25 Standards Every Inspector Should Know**
  Item Number: 0037

- **How to Inspect for Moisture Intrusion**
  Item Number: 0073

- **International Standards of Practice for Inspecting Commercial Properties**
  Item Number: 0016

- **Structural Issues for Home Inspectors**
  Item Number: 0059

The purpose of these publications is to provide accurate and useful information for home inspectors in order to perform an inspection of the various systems at a residential property. They also serve as study aids for InterNACHI's online courses, as well as reference manuals for on the job.

Find these books plus more tools to grow your inspection business at
www.InspectorOutlet.com

INSPECTOR OUTLET

YOU'LL BE SHOCKED AT OUR LOW PRICES!

Inspector Outlet is your source for all things home inspection-related. We are the official store for InterNACHI publications, equipment and apparel. We strive to provide the best products at the lowest prices in the industry.

Find an outstanding selection of original training manuals, checklists, articles and PDFs, as well as publications for clients, including the best-selling home-maintenance guide, *Now That You've Had a Home Inspection*.

We offer a great line of protective outerwear and customized apparel for home inspectors, including shirts, jackets and hats.

InterNACHI's Inspector Marketing Department can design and print a variety of custom marketing materials for your home inspection business.

Protect yourself and your clients on the job with our specialized safety and inspection equipment that help make your inspections easier and safer.

Are you an InterNACHI member? Inspector Outlet offers free inspector decals and embroidered patches to all eligible members!

"Inspector Outlet is officially endorsed by InterNACHI for the best prices in the business for our members."
—Nick Gromicko, Founder of InterNACHI

INSPECTOR OUTLET

www.InspectorOutlet.com   Sales@InspectorOutlet.com